LEAFSABOMINATION

DAVE FESCHUK *&* MICHAEL GRANGE

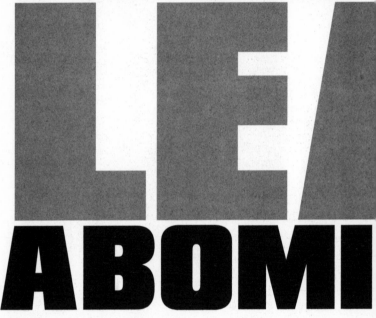

LE/

ABOMI

LFS
NATION

THE DISMAYED FAN'S HANDBOOK TO WHY THE LEAFS STINK AND HOW THEY CAN RISE AGAIN

 RANDOM HOUSE CANADA

www.randomhouse.ca

Random House Canada and colophon are registered trademarks

Library and Archives Canada Cataloguing in Publication

Feschuk, Dave
Leafs abomiNation : the dismayed fans' handbook to
why the Leafs stink and how they can rise again / Dave
Feschuk, Michael Grange.

ISBN 978-0-307-35776-2

1. Toronto Maple Leafs (Hockey team).
I. Grange, Michael II. Title.

GV848.T6F47 2009   796.962'6409713541   C2009-901815-2

Design by Andrew Roberts

Page 253 constitutes an extension of this copyright page

Printed in the United States of America

10 9 8 7 6 5 4 3 2

To our families

CONTENTS

Stephen Harper's Index

[In Honour of Canada's 22nd Prime Minister, a Toronto-born right winger and suspected Leafs fan who has long vowed to write a book about hockey, with apologies to Harper's Index]

Number of Stanley Cups won by Toronto's NHL franchise since it became known as the Maple Leafs in 1927: 11

Number of Stanley Cups won by Toronto's NHL franchise when they were known as the Arenas and the St. Patricks, when the league consisted of four teams: 2

Number of Stanley Cups won by Detroit's NHL franchise since it became known as the Red Wings in 1932: 11

Number of Stanley Cups won by the Red Wings in the post-1967-expansion NHL: 4

Number of Stanley Cups won by the Montreal Canadiens: 24

Number of Stanley Cups won by the Canadiens post-expansion: 10

Number of Stanley Cups won by the Leafs post-expansion: 0

Number of times a Leaf won the Norris Trophy as the NHL's top defenceman since it was first awarded in 1954: 0

Number of times a Boston Bruin won the Norris Trophy: 13

Number of times a member of the other four Original Six teams won the Norris Trophy: 28

Number of times a Leaf finished runner-up in voting for the Norris Trophy: 6

Number of Leafs who have won a major NHL trophy since 1993, when Doug Gilmour won the Selke Trophy as top defensive forward and Pat Burns won the Adams Trophy as coach of the year: 0

Number of Leafs who won a major NHL trophy between Dave Keon's capturing of the Conn Smythe as playoff MVP in 1967 and 1993: 0

Number of seasons in which a Leaf has scored 100-plus points since the franchise's founding: 3

Number of 100-point scorers on the 1985–86 Edmonton Oilers: 4

Number of times a Leaf has finished among the NHL's top 10 scorers since 1967: 15

Number of times a member of the Boston Bruins has been among the top 10 in the same time period: 44

Number of times an NHL player has scored 50 or more goals in a season: 185

Number of times a Leaf has notched 50 or more in a season: 5

Number of times the Leaf who scored 50 was Rick Vaive: 3

Career NHL points by Jeff Ware, Toronto's first-round pick (15th overall) in the 1995 entry draft: 1

Number of players selected by other teams after Ware who scored a minimum 200 NHL points: 13

Number of players selected by other teams after Ware who played a minimum 300 NHL games: 31

Number of combined NHL points scored by the nine players selected by the Leafs in the 1999 entry draft, none of which were scored by 24th-overall pick Luca Cereda: 1

Career NHL points scored by Brad Boyes, the most by a Leafs draft pick from 1999 to 2009: 245

Points scored by Boyes for the Leafs: 0

**Average number of career NHL points scored by the
16 first-round draft picks of the Ottawa Senators
from 1992 to 2006: 233**

Number of consecutive seasons the Leafs have missed the playoffs,
a franchise record: 4

**Franchise record for consecutive seasons out of the playoffs
by the Montreal Canadiens: 3**

Number of general managers employed by each of
the Detroit Red Wings and New Jersey Devils during the 14–
season span from 1995 to 2009 in which the two clubs won a
combined seven Stanley Cups: 1

**Number of general managers employed by the Leafs over the
same time period (counting Cliff Fletcher twice): 6**

Number of times during the 2008-09 season the Leafs
presented Stephen Harper with a No. 1 Toronto jersey in which
he declined to be photographed: 1

It's a Stanley Cup parade in Toronto. Remember that one when people were throwing ribbons and cheering and...oh, you don't?

Introduction

"Listen, I'm tired, and sick and (f***ing) tired about having (f***ing) people that won't come to the (f***ing) rink and you have to (f***king) ask people to get shook up and you have got to ask people to get moving around and you have to (f***ing) try to motivate people. I gotta figure that we gotta (f***ing) seriously, (god***n), consider what the (f**k) we got on this hockey club. And they're not (f***ing) fooling nobody. And most of all, they're not fooling anybody else in the (f***ing) league. They (f***ing) let a guy (f***ing) run Borje Salming at the end of the (f***ing) game and never do (f**k) all. It's a disgrace. I'm sick and (f***ing) tired of making excuses on all these (f***ing) guys that's getting paid on this hockey club blaming somebody else all the (f***ing) time."

—*John Brophy, Leafs coach, 1988*

It's one of the sporting world's seemingly eternal questions: How can it be that Toronto's once-mighty National Hockey League franchise, staggering decrepitly towards its ninety-third birthday, hasn't won a Stanley Cup since the year it turned fifty? How is it that the

Toronto Maple Leafs, with their iconic sweaters and their all-weather fan base and their bottomless coffers and their dynastic tradition, have been reduced to a punchline? How can it be, in an era in which bruised and bearded playoff warriors have been sipping from the Cup in ice-averse places like North Carolina, Florida and California, that the team that plays in the self-proclaimed centre of the hockey universe just spent its fourth straight season experiencing the thrill of post-season hockey as spectators rather than combatants—the longest playoff drought in the team's tempestuous history?

Grab a coffee. Sit back. There is plenty of blame to go around.

Blame the current majority owner, the Ontario Teachers' Pension Plan, which amounts to a faceless pile of money representing the retirement savings of thousands of schoolteachers. Thanks in part to the bullet-proof return on investment supplied by the hapless hockeyists who miraculously turn losses into profits, Ontario's teachers will be spared the indignity of hawking their Dave Keon rookie cards in their golden years, although they may never see a Stanley Cup parade in Toronto. The pension plan's unwelcome intrusion into the sporting realm, where it has treated a cherished public trust as though it's just another widget factory, makes some Leaf fans long occasionally for even the days of the late Harold Ballard. The former owner may have run the team into the ground in 1970s and '80s, but at least he had the courtesy to get sick and die. Pension plans may not be as irascible or as mercurial as Ballard, but they tend to stick around.

Blame the current minority owner, Larry Tanenbaum. As a 20 percent stakeholder, he is not really the owner at all, though that doesn't stop him from treating the dressing room like a real-life version of Facebook, sending friend requests to players young enough to be his grandsons. John Ferguson Jr., the former Leafs general manager, tells a story of the first moment the media became aware that his name had been added to the list of candidates during the club's seemingly eternal GM search in 2003. Ferguson was at the NHL draft in his capacity as the assistant GM of the St. Louis Blues when he spent some time chatting with a member of the Hogtown media.

"The situation in Toronto is [screwed] up," said the reporter, and Ferguson begged him elaborate. "As we speak, Tie Domi is vacationing at Tanenbaum's cottage up north."

Blame the monopoly. The Leafs have been the only big-league hockey ticket in town for most of a century now. The Buffalo Sabres, who reside some 140 kilometres down the QEW, are close enough to host de facto home games for the Leafs (not that they ever win in Buffalo). Toronto's southern Ontario fan base has traditionally swarmed across the border for the Queen City's cheaper tickets and chicken wings, but the Sabres are far enough away to pose no actual competition for hearts or disposable incomes. And while economists will tell you that every empire eventually falls—that every monopoly comes to destroy itself through the arrogance and complacency created by an absence of a rival in the market— what they can't tell you is how long the hubristic Leafs might spend descending toward that fate. The Roman Empire, remember, left its helpless minions ruing their lot in life for most of five centuries. This could go on for a while.

Blame their general managers and their scouts. Generations of so-called brain trusts have, as a group, drafted like drunken hockey-pool noodlers. Between 1992 and 2006, their thirteen first-round picks produced an average of 82 career points each, ranking in the bottom third of the league. And for the most part their trades have been even worse than their draft picks. Gord Stellick, to cite one particularly memorable example of poor judgment by a Toronto GM, helped begin his transition from an NHL executive to the excellent radio-show host that he is today by swapping Russ Courtnall, one of the Leafs' more successful first-round picks over the years, for troubled pugilist John Kordic, who was later traded to Washington for a fifth-round pick before he died in a cocaine haze.

Leaf decision-makers just seem to have no talent for assessing talent. And for a while, when they could outspend their competitors, when the city boomed and ticket prices ballooned, they could get away with those impairments. Cliff Fletcher could wave a hand in disdain and say, "Draft, schmaft"—as he did in the 1990s, when, to his credit, he had put together the best team Toronto has seen in the post-1967 era. And the horns still honked for post-season victories in April and May on the streets of the GTA. But their lust for short-term success and inability to navigate the economic order that emerged in the wake of the cancelled 2004–05 season have chronically inhibited the team's ability to assemble a roster chock full of young talent.

Blame bad coaching. Of the sixteen men who've come and gone as head coach of the Leafs since the team's last championship, more than half of them, ten to be exact, never coached again in the NHL. Of those who moved on to other jobs and are no longer active, only Pat Burns and Roger Neilson managed to put together a winning record in their post-Toronto careers. Hogtown starts to look like the anti-New York: if you can't make it there, you probably can't make it anywhere.

Blame yourself, too. Or, if you're exempt from Leafian love, blame the fans who put up with not only the nonsense on the ice, but also the most expensive ticket prices in the NHL. The consumer behaviour of the fans in blue and white seems to defy the laws of economics, but is not technically unique. The drinkers of civet coffee, for instance, the world's most expensive joe at more than $50 a cup, insist on grinding beans that have passed through the digestive tracts of cat-like Asian mammals— steaming proof that Leafs fans, as much as they're derided as suckers, aren't alone in paying ridiculous prices for crap.

Blame the lame celebrity fans, among them Stephen Harper (who grew up in Toronto and won't admit to his allegiance, yet sniffs the Leaf jock-strap every chance he gets) and Mike Myers, the Scarborough Hollywood star who made a movie about the Leafs, *The Love Guru,* and only exposed his beloved team to more widespread abuse. "Probably the funniest thing about Mike Myers' misfired 'comedy' is the idea that the Toronto Maple Leafs could win the Stanley Cup," chirped the *Winnipeg Free Press.* Nice job, Mr. *Wayne's World*—not! Or blame the corporations who've turned Toronto hockey games into what amounts to a business meeting, helping to inflate ticket prices by exploiting a perfectly legal tax write-off. Blame the suits, indeed, for turning a supposedly exciting hockey game into something as quiet and solemn and hopeless as a getaway to prison.

And blame the Leafs—the players themselves—none of whom have been good enough to win, say, a scoring title or a Hart or a Vezina or a Calder or a Norris Trophy since the glory-less drought began. The laws of probability would seem to suggest that all these years and millions of dollars of payroll would have seen a bona fide NHL star suit up in the blue and white. It's not easy to see why Torontonians are still waiting, though there is no shortage of theories. Leaf players can't excel, the open-line callers opine, because Toronto is too easy or too hard a place to play; because the millionaires don't want to leave their Forest Hill mansions and their Muskoka summer homes; because every fourth-liner is a night-club A-lister; because the pressure's stifling and the puck bunnies are higher-maintenance than you'd think. "If there's a little cock to our walk, it's not so much our doing," Darcy Tucker once said, back when the Leafs were a playoff team. "Walk down the street and people are hugging you like you're a movie star."

Blame all the unconscionable perpetrators mentioned above—we certainly do. But understand too that there is some measure of hope, and that it arrived at 40 Bay Street on November 28, 2008. That's when Brian Burke was introduced as the twelfth general manager in Leafs history. That's when the graduate of Harvard's law school, who'd celebrated a Stanley Cup as the general manager of the Anaheim Ducks only a couple of years earlier, was handed the keys to a beautiful fifteenth-floor office, a six-year contract that was said to pay him approximately triple what he had earned in California, and a roster full of not-ready-for-prime-time lightweights.

If you were doing the math, you'll know that Burke was taking to the lectern to announce his vision for the team on Day 15,187, precisely forty-one years, six months and twenty-seven days since the Leafs were last presented with the Lord Stanley of Preston's chalice and goaltending hero Terry Sawchuk smoked a celebratory cigarette between gulps of stubby-bottled beer as he mugged for the cameras. And if there is still optimism, it is balanced with cynicism. Earnest cheers of "Go Leafs Go!" have turned, for some, to fed-up mock-chants of "Golf Leafs Golf!" In twenty-six seasons of the forty-three since the Leafs last celebrated a championship, the club has either missed the playoffs or lost in the first round. Only four times have Toronto's hopefuls advanced to the championship semifinals, and each time, it goes without saying, they've been defeated. While the Chicago Blackhawks, who haven't touched the Cup since 1961, have the shameful distinction of being the NHL team with the longest streak of futility, they have at least been to a final in the interim (they've been there five times, actually, losing in the seventh game twice). In their chronic failure the Leafs have tarnished the proud tradition established by Conn Smythe, the Maple Leafs patriarch who, on Valentine's Day, 1927, fronted a group that bought the franchise formerly known as the St. Patricks and lived to see his name inscribed on the Cup eight times.

Burke, an Irishman like Smythe, was reverent in his opening remarks to the press.

"You're talking about the Vatican if you're a Catholic," he said of his new place of work (while Smythe, a Protestant who distrusted Catholics, surely pounded a fist into the soil at Park Lawn Cemetery on the other side of town). "You're talking about the centre of the hockey universe. You're talking about one of the most important jobs in hockey on the planet, running the Toronto Maple Leafs. It's a dream job. I couldn't be more excited to be here today. I couldn't be more excited about the job that lies ahead. This is one of the crown jewels in the National Hockey League. It's an iconic brand worldwide. And for someone to turn to you and say, 'We want you to run this team,' it's just like a dream come true . . .

"When I was first offered the job I probably embarrassed myself how quickly I said I wanted to take this job. That's how badly I wanted it."

What was he going to do with it?

Burke, as he eased into his tone-setting address to Leafs Nation, announced that he'd build his team on "three pillars." Three pillars? Was Burke advocating some sort of return to the "pyramid power" of Red Kelly, the 1970s Leafs coach who took the unusual step of channeling the supernatural energy of Egyptian polygons by putting pyramids in the dressing room and under the bench (with some success, it should be noted; it was with a pyramid-blessed stick that Darryl Sittler scored ten points in a single game in 1976)? No, Burke had something else in mind.

Pillar One, pronounced Burke: "We play an entertaining style. We want to justify the price of the ticket every night, whether the team is successful that night or not. We believe in aggressive pursuit of the puck in all three zones, or possession of it desirably. We believe in answering the physical challenge and playing a style that allows your young players to play and develop in a fear-free environment. That's number one."

Pillar Two: "We believe in financial and fiscal prudence," said Burke.

And bingo! Now everybody in the building knew exactly why CEO Richard Peddie had seemed so sold on Burke from the get-go. "It's not my money," said Burke as he explained his fiduciary duty, "so I try to spend it as wisely as I can." Few in attendance seemed to bat an eyelash as Burke bowed at the feet of the bottom line so early in his address. But here he was, kissing the hand-sewn Italian loafers of the bean counters even as he spoke to the fans of a team owned by a succession of parties who have rightfully been accused of caring far more about their return on investment than their hockey team's return to glory.

And Pillar Three ("a commitment to community service") won't help the cause, unless you believe Bobby Orr dominated the NHL in the 1970s because he made good-hearted visits to the children's wards of New England hospitals. So, two pillars, really. Try to win, sure. But definitely make money. From the fan's point of view, however, is the right objective taking priority?

But enough with the skepticism for now. Burke, for all his rough edges, has done it before (although one wonders if he mentioned in his job interview, as he did at his opening press conference, that he'd lucked into signing Scott Niedermayer, the Ducks defenceman who was named the MVP of Anaheim's Cup-winning run in 1997, because Scott's brother Rob was already a member of the team and the pair wished to play together). And there are those who'll suggest, in this book's coming chapters, that Burke might just have the fortitude to withstand the pressure to produce night-to-night success in a city whose hockey teams have suffered in the face of a pretty much annual surrender to instant gratification. There is hope too in the law of probabilities, which promise that just as even the blind squirrel feasts on the occasional nut, and NASCAR fans in North Carolina might be bewildered from time to time by a Stanley Cup parade, so too might Leaf fans pin their hopes on the possibility that their turn will come, despite everything. And there is hope, too, if not in pyramid power, then in the rhythmic and seemingly inevitable progressions in the universe of sports that take so many teams from worst to first, from basement to penthouse, and maybe one particular team from AbomiNation to recapturing imaginations.

As long as the Leafs are playing hockey, and as long as Leaf fans are Leaf fans, there will be hope. You're still a Leaf fan, there are still Leaf fans, because Hogtown and its environs have maybe never been more electric than they were in 1993, when Wendel Clark pounded Marty McSorley and the Buds were a game away from a rematch of the 1967 Habs-Leafs final. Because if Kerry Fraser, blind as a bat, had tossed Gretzky from that game six for high-sticking Dougie Gilmour for four stitches, as he should have, franchise-decimating books like this one wouldn't have nearly the same oomph. Because that jersey, even with all the Ballard-era tinkering and the recent jarring removal of the torso striping, is still a classic. Because, for all the talk of soccer and basketball taking over the world—and nobody's saying they're not great games—you've been Guy Number 31 in a 36-guy shinny game on a sunny day on the slushy ice at the outdoor rink at Dufferin Grove or Withrow Park or Barbara Ann Scott, and you know hockey lives in our cold bones. Because, to steal the words and the form from Dave Bidini, the hockey nomad and Leafs diehard who wrote "Blueblood," a mini-essay almost beautiful enough to make a Habs fan convert, "winning is just losing minus the numbers." Because Peddie, for all his corporate-catchphrase-parroting, Porsche-driving, Armani-suit-wearing ridiculousness, might be a good enough marketer to extract the last loonie from your pocket lint, but he can't sap your love for the game.

Owner Harold Ballard was delighted at the number of paying customers at a Leafs home game. And at the absence of Russians in his team's lineup.

Chapter One
Blame History

"The Toronto Maple Leafs haven't won a Stanley Cup since 1967 and I thought the only way I'll probably see a Stanley Cup in my lifetime is if I write it."

—Mike Myers, writer, director and star of The Love Guru,
a box-office bomb of a comedy wherein the Leafs finally win

IMAGINE A LITTLE KID growing up in a dilapidated row-house in a joyless city crowded with horse-drawn carriages and pony-carts. His father is a teetotalling vegetarian and failed businessman. His mother has drunk herself to death at the tender age of thirty-eight. The kid is a scrapper and a go-getter. No, this is not the opening chapter of a long-lost Charles Dickens novel. It is the childhood of Leafs patriarch Conn Smythe.

The Smythe family lived on North Street, a stretch of road north of Bloor that is today part of Bay Street, only a few city blocks up the hill from where the Air Canada Centre now sits. Far removed from the luxury

suites and on-demand shrimp of the pampered generations to come, Smythe's was a hardscrabble existence in
a hard era. "The greatest fight I ever saw was one day
going home from school when a fight started between
three St. Mike's kids," Smythe enthused in his autobiography, referring to the Catholic boys' school. "One
fought the other two up a lane and then along street after
street, always with his back to the wall, or he never would
have been able to hang on. It was a lesson I didn't forget:
if you looked after your rear, you could keep going. It
works in fights, war, business." Smythe's trademark phrase
would come to be among the most famous quotations in
hockey history. "If you can't beat 'em in the alley," went
a mantra that doubled as the title of his posthumously
published memoir, "you can't beat 'em on the ice."

Clawing to carve out a legacy and a fortune, Smythe
left marks you could still see long after he died in 1980.
Smythe didn't drink, citing his mother's addiction as
his reason for abstinence. Maple Leaf Gardens, perhaps
at least partly because of the great builder's feelings on
the evils of the sauce—and certainly because of Toronto's
well-earned reputation as a conservative burg that tolerated fun only in small doses—didn't serve beer until
1993. If today's Leafs crowds are castigated for their
sit-upon-hands reserve, blame Smythe for setting the
tone. In a time before the sideboards were topped with
Plexiglas, Smythe was said to strut along them in his
spats, peering down and inspecting the wardrobe of the

season-ticket holders and generally ensuring order. But then, his walkabouts may have been no more than keeping an eye on the rabble. During the years when Smythe ruled the Gardens, a Toronto police officer once told a newspaperman that illegal activity declined significantly on the nights of Leafs games. The implication seems to be that if the people running the Gardens were a bunch of crooks, so were the fans.

If he came off as holier-than-thou—and almost everything you can read about him suggests he was among the more insufferable and self-righteous men to occupy a seat of power in the sports sphere—politely acknowledge your respect for his sacrifice as a veteran of both World Wars. He was captured by the Germans in the First World War and wounded badly in the Second, absorbing a burst of shrapnel that caused him no end of pain until his dying day. He was also the benefactor of a charitable foundation that still raises boatloads of money to help children with disabilities. The Conn Smythe Dinner remains a fixture on the social calendars of the Toronto sports community.

But Smythe had warts that belonged to his era just as much as his heroism and philanthropy. He, like all NHL owners of his day as a rule, underpaid his players while pocketing massive profits. "I never shared things well with anybody, all my life," he once admitted, albeit referring to his sister, for whom he had little time. He wasn't above cheating; he acknowledged in his memoir that he'd once been a party to attempting to fix a horse-race at Toronto's old Hillcrest racetrack. He had a fear and disdain of Jews and Catholics that makes Don Cherry's hate-on for French Canadians and Europeans seem downright quaint. "We sincerely believed if we were captured by the priests, we'd never be seen alive again," Smythe wrote in his autobiography. "I've always thought that Catholics have it pretty easy—do anything they like, then confess, and be forgiven. It's the opposite of, 'as ye sow, so shall ye reap.' I know that there is no such thing as being forgiven." And indeed, he held grudges. Long of the opinion that one of his best players, Busher Jackson, was a disgrace to the game because Jackson was said to enjoy women and alcohol more than most, Smythe lobbied tirelessly to keep Jackson out of the Hall of Fame, going as far to resign as the Hall's president when Jackson was finally inducted.

Armed with only limited experience with a handful of amateur hockey teams for which he'd played and coached, Smythe landed the GM's job with the New York Rangers in 1926 on little more than a friend's recommendation. Smythe used his knowledge of the Canadian hinterlands to put together a roster that would win the Stanley Cup in 1928, but not before the Rangers would relieve him of his managerial duties in favour of Lester Patrick. Smythe took his severance pay along with some gambling winnings and cobbled together a group of investors to buy the Toronto St. Patricks.

Legend has it that he also talked the previous ownership out of accepting a higher bid from a buyer that
intended to move the team to Philadelphia by appealing
to the Torontonians' civic pride (whether the pre-Smythe
owners did Toronto a favour or a disservice depends on
your outlook). Either way, showing civic pride meant
showing a remarkable profit. The four men who sold the
team to Smythe's group—one of whom, J.P. Bickell,
retained his stake in the club—had bought it a few years
earlier for a measly $5,000. On February 14, 1927, they
allowed it to be taken off their hands for $160,000.
Precisely two years later, seven gangsters in Al Capone's
Chicago would be gunned down in a mass slaying that
would become known as the St. Valentine's Day Massacre.
Call the sale of the St. Patricks, with its 1,600 percent cash
return, a plain old St. Valentine's Day Killing. From the
beginning, Toronto's NHL franchise has carved out a reputation for providing its overseers with exponential riches.

Smythe, with money on his mind, understood the
team needed a more universally appealing image, one
that wasn't so specifically catholic in origin. In short
order, he changed the colours from green and white to
blue and white, and changed the name to the Maple
Leafs (leaving it to generations of parents to explain to
their kids why their heroes weren't "Leaves"—though
often a target of rival fans' mockery, the name was
already in use by other Toronto sports teams; Merriam-
Webster's dictionary even today considers "leafs" a valid

pluralization of "leaf"). He also understood the necessity of a grander stage than the 8,000-seat Mutual Street Arena in which the St. Pats (and their previous incarnation, the Arenas) had played since the NHL's founding in 1917. A few years into his tenure as the team's owner, he undertook the unlikely project of building what would become, for a couple of generations, the country's best-known building. Maple Leaf Gardens was built in a flurry in the throes of the Dirty Thirties against almost all logic and a backdrop of grim prognostications.

As Foster Hewitt, the game's very voice, would later write: "When Maple Leaf Gardens was only an idea the critics said, 'You can't finance it.' When the plans were drawn the doubters declared, 'You can't have it ready for opening night.' When the building was completed the pessimists prophesied, 'You can't fill it.' But every prediction was false, for on November 12, 1931, the largest crowd in Toronto's history to witness an indoor event of any kind packed into the new ice palace."

The story goes that Smythe coveted a bedrock player to build a champion around. He recognized that King Clancy, the gutsy defenceman who'd been at the heart of the Ottawa Senators' Stanley Cup wins in 1923 and 1927, was that man. Smythe also knew he was short of the cash that would be required to secure Clancy. By this time, the irascible owner had gone from simply betting on horse races to owning racehorses. He had a filly, Rare Jewel, running in the Coronation Futurity at Woodbine and, in a gamble to meet the Clancy price, he bet heavily on her despite the fact that she was a 100-to-1 shot. Whether it was improbably good luck, or another instance of the uncanny Smythe arranging the outcome at the racetrack, as he was not above doing, Rare Jewel won the race, Smythe won almost $15,000, and Clancy became a Leaf. Perhaps it was both good luck and shrewd planning. What's for sure is that Smythe, as the controlling owner and effective general manager, had more luck or skill or both at building Maple Leaf rosters than almost every other man who'd inhabit the role.

The Clancy-led Leafs—teamed with Red Horner, Hap Day, Lorne Chabot, et al, and with Dick Irvin as coach—won the Cup in Clancy's second year in Toronto, the team's first season at the Gardens. The teams Smythe governed would win six of ten Stanley Cups from 1942 to 1951, and plenty of glorious lore would be etched in the winning. The 1942 Leafs, for instance, coached by Day and captained by Syl Apps, became the first pro sports team to come back from a 3-0 series deficit to win a best-of-seven series, defeating the Detroit Red Wings in four straight elimination games to win the Cup. (That feat wouldn't be matched until the 1975 New York Islanders came back from three games down to the Pittsburgh Penguins to reach the final).

How'd they pull it off?

"It was pretty easy to get up for every game in the old days," said Gordie Drillon, a member of that Leafs squad. "You know how we got up? Mr. Smythe would walk in the dressing room and reach in his pocket and hold up three tickets. He'd say, 'See this? There are three going to [the farm club in] Syracuse tonight and three coming back." If you think Ron Wilson is a cruel taskmaster for sitting Jason Blake for a few shifts or skating his squad without pucks after a loss, keep in mind that Wilson would come off like a kindly uncle in the Smythe regime.

Smythe's Leafs weren't prima donnas, but they were stars, albeit in a different age. Back when the NHL was a select club of some 120 players (compared with today's approximately 700), the Leafs were a perennial power-house. A Toronto player led the league in scoring for six of the seven seasons between 1931 to 1938, Drillon racking up 52 points in 48 games to top the chart. Who could have predicted then that Drillon would still be the last Leaf to win the scoring title more than two decades after his death in 1986?

But there was still a steady stream of talent filing into Maple Leaf Gardens every autumn. Between Syl Apps in 1937 and Brit Selby in 1966, Toronto players won more of their fair share of Calder Trophies, awarded to the NHL's top rookie each spring. They piled up nine over that span, or nearly double the average in a six-team league. Though Calder-winners Gaye Stewart and Kent Douglas may not be household names anymore, Dave Keon and Frank Mahovlich certainly are, as is

Howie Meeker, who was fresh from the war effort when he won the trophy in 1947.

How good were those Leaf teams? The 1945 edition finished twenty-eight points behind Montreal in the standings, but ended up beating them in an epic six-game semifinal en route to winning the Cup yet again.

But Smythe was not running a charity devoted to the health of Toronto's sense of community spirit. "[Leafs] management has always been business-conscious," Foster Hewitt wrote in 1955. "No enterprise could have a directorate that reads like the all-star team of Canadian financial leaders without being dollar-minded. Conservatively managed, it has steadily improved its position . . .

"From an investment point of view the Gardens have done remarkably well. In one of its early years the club offered one of its players $3,000 in currency plus $3,000 in stock for a season's salary. 'Nothing doing,' the player declared. 'I want it all in money.' The player was paid as he preferred, but if he had taken the stock and retained it for a few years he would have received over $30,000 for his initial $3,000."

Smythe's return on investment as the Leafs' owner was even more impressive. In 1961, Smythe sold the majority stake in the Gardens for some $2.3 million, claiming that he was essentially handing down the club—albeit hardly gifting it—to his son Stafford. Though the elder Smythe must have known his son couldn't have come up with enough money to buy the team on his own, the Leafs' first owner expressed public shock that Stafford was in cahoots with a couple of members of the club's board of directors, John Bassett and Harold Ballard.

From that moment, of course, everything changed. It changed on the ice because the fact remains that Conn Smythe's Leafs, or Leafs teams that consisted of players he brought to the team, won eleven Stanley Cups, and the post-Conn Smythe Leafs have won none.

And it changed off the ice, too. The transaction would be the beginning of the end of the Smythe family's influence on the club Conn built. Years later, Stafford Smythe's son Thomas would allege that Ballard crowbarred the Smythe family out of the ownership picture forever by tricking a drunken Stafford into signing an altered will that paved the way for Ballard to take control of the Gardens. And even more recently, with the Gardens all but forgotten and Maple Leaf Sports and Entertainment—MLSE, the Leafs, Raptors and Toronto FC ownership conglomerate—long in control, members of the Smythe family complained publicly that they were no longer invited to the Air Canada Centre's directors' lounge.

But the changes began long before that, when Ballard and Bassett and Stafford Smythe began to have their way. Profits tripled in short order, but heads shook, too. The Gardens was suddenly awash in advertising. And crowded with new seats too. While the elder Smythe took pity on the throngs of Leaf fans standing three- and four-deep in the arena's upper reaches and actually reduced the number of tickets sold per game from 16,318 to 14,500, the new regime set about jamming new seats into crevices once thought too tiny. The old patriarch justified the loss in revenue on the grounds that "it isn't fair to sell standing tickets to folks who can't see the ice. . . . We will cut our ticket sales and give everyone a chance to have a look at the play."

But his son and his pals had no such compunction. Old seats were shaved smaller. The portrait of the Queen that hung at one end was removed in the name of yet more ticket revenue. Scott Young, the sportswriter who would co-author Conn Smythe's autobiography a couple of decades later, assessed the new Leafs ownership back in the 1960s in words that seem eerily relevant today: "They've removed the sentiment from the operation."

Sniffed the *Globe* magazine in 1966: "The word is that the Gardens has fallen into the clutches of a naughty and mercenary trio of upstarts who have no regard for a sacred trust and are interested only in making money." Sportswriters don't really use the word "naughty" all that much anymore, but the idea hasn't changed.

🍁

HAROLD BALLARD, of course, would ultimately emerge as the lone majority owner, and "the Ballard Years" would enter the annals of Toronto hockey lore as the name of the era in which the mighty Leafs began their dizzying descent towards the status of laughingstock, a mantle they will probably only shrug off by winning a Stanley Cup. If that goal seems impossibly distant today, it is in large part a consequence of the venality, capriciousness and shortsightedness that marked the lost years between 1972 and Ballard's long-awaited death in 1990.

Money, of course, was at the heart of the sickness that infected the Leafs after Conn Smythe gave up the reins. Stafford Smythe was also charged with plundering the Gardens' treasury, though he would die before the trial at age fifty. (Bassett would eventually bow out after repeated disagreements with Ballard.) And at one point Ballard found himself running the club from a minimum-security prison outside Kingston, where he was doing time after being convicted of using the publicly traded Gardens' money as if it were his own. He was found guilty of forty-eight counts of fraud and theft, but he was never brought before a judge for running the Leafs into the ground.

Ballard's anything-for-a-buck lust knew few boundaries. Concerned about a loss in revenue from program sales when the NHL mandated that teams emblazon jerseys with the players' surnames, Ballard obeyed the ordinance to the letter: he saw to it that white letters were sewn on the backs of white jerseys, so fans couldn't possibly read them. He sold the Stanley Cup banners that hung from the Gardens rafters. He once made inquiries with the arena superintendent as to how many cucumbers would fit in the 30,000-gallon tank that held the mixture that circulated through the refrigeration pipes beneath the rink floor. "He said he wanted to make dill pickles to sell at games," rink manager Wayne Gilespie told the authors of the book *Forever Rivals*. "He'd dream up these schemes—anything to make a buck—then he'd forget about them."

Part petulant mogul, part malicious buffoon, Ballard seemed capable of just about anything. His quirks were many. A speedboat racer in his youth, in his old age, when he lived in an apartment in the Gardens and would occasionally stumble into employees wearing only his underwear, Ballard was said to occasionally indulge in the sport of nude Zamboni driving. And his bluster was often beyond belief—no surprise from a man who counted "Bullshit baffles brains" among his favourite maxims. "Pal Hal," as he was known by those who admired him—and there are always willing admirers of sports owners, no matter how wayward or bizarre the honcho may be—once promised to trade his entire team. Another time, he chalked up centreman Laurie Boschman's slump to the player's faith as a born-again Christian. He called the Soviets "savages," and at one point barred them from his building. He called players who defected from the Eastern bloc "traitors," yet still employed them. He banned women from the locker room, defying league rules and common sense. "Women will be allowed to go in the locker room if they undress first," Ballard quipped. He once tussled in a phone interview with Barbara Frum, the esteemed CBC radio broadcaster, punctuating the call with an assertion that women belonged "on their back." When journalist William Houston informed him of his intention to write his biography, Ballard approached Houston after a game in Chicago in 1984 and said, "If there's one word about me, you'll get your throat cut." Houston wrote the book and lived to retire from his job as a *Globe and Mail* columnist some twenty-five years later, though that should not be taken to mean that Ballard got along well with reporters, or even that he wanted to. The team's media guide described him as "one of the most loved and most hated people in Canada" and "master promoter and manipulator of the media."

But writing about Ballard was a walk in the park compared to being related to him. His youngest son, Harold Jr., was once arrested for breaking and entering at his father's family home—after old Harold had kicked the boy to the curb. In another tender family moment, Ballard cancelled a peewee tournament scheduled to take place in the Gardens when he discovered that his estranged daughter's son (yes, his grandson) was on the roster of one of the teams. And his oldest son, Bill, was once fired by his dad from the Gardens board. But then, Bill had his own role to play in the family drama. In 1989 he was convicted of assaulting his father's "companion," Yolanda, whose place in Leafs lore would come to be recorded with the kind of contempt usually reserved for Yoko Ono or Tammy Faye Bakker.

She had previously pled guilty to charges of conspiracy to commit fraud and perjury after it was alleged she had schemed with an accomplice to bilk a wealthy ageing man of some $3 million by altering the old sod's will. Ballard once accused Yolanda of "trying to pull the same thing on me." And indeed she may have. In 1987 she did legally change her name to Ballard from MacMillan, though she and her bumptious paramour never did tie the knot. In fact, while Ballard was recovering from a heart attack in 1988, he had the locks changed on his home, and had Yolanda's possessions hauled away. Though the ugly soap opera continued until Ballard's death, Yolanda was not invited to the funeral or the reading of the will—thus ensuring that the drama would continue even after he was in the ground. Not to be so easily outmanoeuvred, Yolanda sued the Ballard estate for $381,000 a month, in part, so the rumour goes, on behalf of her dog.

Given Ballard's tempestuous relationship with members of his family, Darryl Sittler should have heard alarm bells go off when the Leafs owner called him "the son I never had." Though Pal Hal never called the police to arrest the best player of the Ballard years, he did trade away heart-and-soul forward Lanny McDonald to the Colorado Rockies in a move deliberately calculated to

upset the Leafs dressing room—and Sittler in particular—
a provocation that worked all too well. Sittler ripped the
captain's "C" from his sweater in protest, and was eventually traded away himself. The Leafs sent their captain,
an eighth-overall pick, Team Canada sniper and prototypical power forward whose name appeared in the
scoring race alongside the likes of Guy Lafleur and Brian
Trottier, to the rival Philadelphia Flyers for some guy
named Rich Costello and a couple of draft picks.

But then, Ballard often treated his coaches and
players with similar disrespect. And the better the player,
the rougher the ride. Dave Keon, the Leafs' perennial
scoring leader, winner of four Stanley Cups in blue and
white and of a Conn Smythe Trophy as most valuable
playoff performer in the Leafs' last Cup run, was not
only not re-signed in Toronto in 1975—he was essentially barred from playing anywhere else in the NHL
because Ballard was demanding so much in compensa-
tion from any team that signed him that other teams
had no choice but to shy away. Keon ended up suiting up
for the Minnesota Fighting Saints of the World Hockey
Association, and had little difficulty lighting up the new
league. But when the franchise ran into financial trouble,
and Keon tried to get back into the NHL, Ballard, who
still controlled his rights, blocked him once again. He
finally ended up playing out his career with the Hartford
Whalers, but only after Ballard had killed a deal between
Keon and the Cup-contending New York Islanders.

To this day, the Hall-of-Famer who was ranked 69th out of the top 100 players of all time by *The Hockey News* in 1998 still has nothing but contempt for the team that has botched not only its own legacy so badly, but also the lives and careers of its players. Thanks, Harold Ballard.

Could any team survive a meddling owner who goes out of his way to squander the likes of Lanny McDonald, Darryl Sittler and Dave Keon in exchange for little more than a pair of Cooperalls? Ballard's own history shows the kind of effect the guy could have on a hockey team. Before he began systematically stripping the Leafs of their intimidating reputation and their best players, Ballard coached an amateur team, the Toronto Sea Fleas, taking over behind the bench after Harry Watson stepped down in 1932. Ballard acknowledged he "didn't know any more about coaching a hockey team than Saint Peter knows about African golf."

"Dress up the Keystone Kops in hockey uniforms, throw in several scenes from the movie *Slap Shot* and you get an idea of what Ballard's attempt at coaching a hockey team was like," wrote William Houston. Sounds a lot like his work as a behind-the-scenes general manager too.

The Sea Fleas might not have done much worse in the NHL than the Leafs if Ballard had sent them over the boards. Toronto fans are disappointed that their team missed the playoffs yet again in the spring of 2009, but at least they won some games over the course of the season. The 1987–88 version of the team actually went fifteen straight games without a victory and ended the campaign going 1–8 to wind up with a .325 winning percentage (though, since the Norris Division was so weak that year, they actually ended up making the play-offs, bowing to the Detroit Red Wings in six games). And that dismal season was typical of the Ballard years. Between 1980–81 and 1989–90, the Leafs finished last in their division an incredible eight times.

There was a joke at the time that Leafs goalie Ken Wregget was once so depressed after a bad loss that he tried to put an end to it all by jumping in front of the team bus—only to watch in horror as the bus squeaked between his legs. But everyone knew the problem wasn't Wregget, it was Ballard. When he fell ill, Gardens stock rose. When he recovered, it fell. When he went into the hospital for a quintuple bypass a few months later, it rose again. "We know he has diabetes," a Toronto investor told a reporter as Ballard neared his end. "We know he doesn't follow his diet. We know he's eighty-three. That's why I started buying stock."

❧

WHEN THE GARDENS CONCRETE FLOOR was re-poured in the 1980s, Ballard took the liberty of marking the concrete below centre ice with imprints of his hands and feet, thereby furnishing Leaf fans with a metaphor that happens to be literally true. Ballard really did leave his paw prints all over the franchise. And his meddling quite literally made things worse—the imprints were said to have compromised the quality of the ice for years. And yes, one of the new regime's first acts was to remove Ballard's prints from the concrete of the Gardens ice pad, solving both practical and symbolic problems in fairly short order.

Of course, nothing is that easy. Ballard's will had hardly been read before a byzantine, four-year board-room tumult for control of the Gardens broke out, as friends, enemies, investors and corporations as big as Molson got their elbows up to lay claim to what was still one of the sporting world's great properties, even at the end of the Ballard years. Lawsuits were launched, favours and loyalties were invoked, millions of dollars changed hands, and when the dust settled grocery baron Steve Stavro, a longtime friend of Ballard's, was at the helm. For a while.

Attending a Leafs game these days, of course, you would be forgiven if you came away believing that the club was never associated with a Smythe, let alone a Ballard—a looming personality that could impose his vision on a team and a city for better or worse. The idea of an owner like that—particularly in an era when there is no identifiable owner at all—seems as quaint as tube skates and fans dressed in jackets and ties.

But those are the guys who got the Leafs here, and it seems strange that they are so close to being totally forgotten. Perhaps that is because MLSE sells naming rights to everything in its purview, and doesn't have anything left to name after the owners who stamped the team so completely with their personalities. The arena cannot be named after Conn Smythe (because it's named after an oft-teetering airline), the dressing room cannot be named after Conn Smythe (because the folks at UnderArmor, the sports-gotchies giant, have paid dearly for their share of that real estate, and can hardly be expected to share it), and the media room cannot be named after Harold Ballard, even if it would be an ironic nod (because a telecommunications company, Rogers, holds sway on the nameplate). Perhaps there is a water fountain somewhere in the ACC as yet unnamed, waiting for a plaque. Or a urinal.

It's been suggested a statue be erected to honour Smythe, if not Ballard. But anyone who knows anything about the folks who run the Maple Leafs know they're saving their bronze for a monument to Richard Peddie, the CEO who, in more recent Leafs history, commiserated after a defeat with then-Leafs coach Paul Maurice about a "tough third quarter." One supposes when you operate quarter to quarter, in the fiscal sense of the word, history begins and ends every three months.

THE LEAFS DO IT AGAIN

AUGUST 25, 1977: Harold Ballard is inducted into the Hockey Hall of Fame.

JUNE 9, 1965: With their NHL goalies Terry Sawchuk and Johnny Bower at age 35 and 40, respectively, the Leafs allow the Bruins to pluck Gerry Cheevers, 24, from their minor-league system in the intraleague draft. He'd go on to backstop two Stanley Cup teams and reside in the Hall of Fame.

MARCH 3, 1968: Leafs trade Frank Mahovlich, Pete Stemkowski, Garry Unger and the rights to Carl Brewer to Detroit for Norm Ullman, Paul Henderson, Floyd Smith and Doug Barrie. The outgoing players go on to tally 1,850 points; what comes back yields 848 points. Oh, and Mahovlich goes on to win two Stanley Cups as a member of the Montreal Canadiens.

JUNE 1969: Leafs select Ernie Moser with the ninth-overall pick in the amateur draft. Moser never plays in the NHL, while no fewer than twelve players selected after him, among them Bobby Clarke and Butch Goring, play at least 400 NHL games.

Favourite whipping boy of frustrated Leafs fans, Maple Leaf Sports and Entertainment CEO Richard Peddie talks to someone hovering just over the press.

Chapter Two
Blame Peddie

"Richard Peddie mini-bio: Put in the position of power in 2003. Not a playoff appearance since 2004! Enough said!"

— *David Chinappi, Mississauga*

AFTER A TIME it got to be too much. The calls kept coming. The bile kept spewing. Richard Peddie was used to being kicked around on sports talk radio, dissected by sports columnists, whispered about by the jocks. But this was a little too much. Phone calls at home. Threatening. Lewd. Personal. The police were called. An investigation followed—the calls came from a public phone near a downtown office tower, though no arrests were ever made. Finally, reluctantly, Peddie changed his phone number, de-listed it, made private one small part of his very public life as one of the least-loved men in Canadian sports.

For reasons real if largely unquantifiable, the long-time chief executive officer of MLSE has been the man in the black hat. The mortician making big margins on the funeral. The guy who dared to call the hockey shrine known as Maple Leaf Gardens a dump. He was right, of course. It *was* a dump. But to Leaf fans, it was *their* dump.

In November 2008 MLSE moved their administrative, hockey and basketball offices from the 6th floor of the Air Canada tower to the fifteenth floor. That meant that Peddie would need to use a different elevator bank to get into the ACC, one that took him all the way down to the parking garage, where he would walk over to the ACC elevators and then into the arena. A more direct route is to get off on the ground floor and head out the front door on Bay Street, turn right on the sidewalk and walk to Gate 2A. "Sometimes I have to go outside," he says. "And sometimes I get 'Peddie, you asshole!' It goes with the turf. I can't say I like it, but it goes with the turf. It happens. Not a lot, but enough." The guy making crank calls from that pay phone? He said worse.

It all seems so unfair. In an era when there is so little for Toronto's hockey fans to cheer about, don't they know they have a proven winner in Richard Peddie? After all, this is a guy who has put his name on some serious hardware. As president and CEO of Pillsbury Canada, Peddie took home the vaunted Donald B. McCaskill Award for Marketing Excellence. And while fans and journalists complain that the Leafs don't have a true number-one goalie, or a first-line centre or a dominating stud defenceman, you'd think they would recognize greatness in the front office. For heaven's sake, when Peddie was president and CEO of the Stadium Corporation of Ontario (better known as SkyDome), the building was chosen Stadium of the Year not once or twice, but four times in a row. Who says Peddie can't win?

Certainly not the MLSE bigwigs. "This board has given us a mandate," Peddie explains. "Grow the company. Grow the company and win championships."

He laughs. "We've done one of them."

Hey, one out of two isn't so bad. That's better than the Leafs did in the 2008–09 season, when they had a losing record and finished out of the playoffs for a record fourth straight year. It's better than the .426 record the Raptors put up over the thirteen years of Peddie's stewardship. And it is a lot better than anything Toronto FC has done on the field; MLSE's soccer team finished last and third-last in its first two seasons, missing the playoffs each year. But it did sell out every home game, so Peddie got half his job done.

"I think we've done really well," he beams.

Come hell or high water, Peddie's teams make money, the Leafs more than any other. Even in the most uncertain economy in generations Peddie can state, with confidence, that the Leafs are "not recession-proof, but recession-resistant." He is talking from MLSE's recently renovated offices, where Peddie's corner overlooks Lake Ontario to the south, a panoramic view through 400 square feet of windows—"studies show you're more productive with natural light"—making it bright even on a gloomy day. Shelf space features mementoes from his glittering career in the packaged-goods industry. Seated at one of four grey leather chairs around a coffee table, Peddie can recite evidence of his success running MLSE with disarming ease. "When I joined twelve years ago, we were a basketball team that played in a rented facility and the Leafs were a hockey team that played in an old, decrepit building—iconic but decrepit, not as charming as everyone likes to paint it to this day," says Peddie. "Now, everything has changed."

Like?

He leans back, legs crossed. "Everything. The degree of business sophistication. Everything is tied in. We cross-sell like crazy. Everything is synergistic. Customer-relationship marketing. We have a million-person database. We have a Jumbotron that feeds off our television channels. When we open Maple Leaf Square we will have master controls that can program two blocks. We'll be able to change what's on the videotron outside to what's on the sports bar to what's on inside the arena. It's all one message."

That message seems to be: buy more stuff.

This is an outfit that knows how to move product. *Toronto Star* reporter Rick Westhead recounts how, only hours after Mats Sundin collected his 500th NHL goal midway through the 2006–07 season, "the nylon mesh net that corralled the landmark puck was removed from the Air Canada Centre and shipped to a factory where workers cut it into 2,000 pieces. The small bits of net were mounted on a board next to a photo of Sundin and slipped into a matted frame. In an instant, otherwise worthless scraps of nylon had been transformed into valuable sports memorabilia . . . a process estimated to generate MLSE an additional $40,000 in revenue, almost all profit." Westhead also tells the story of how the Zamboni slush from the final game played at Maple Leaf Gardens was melted, packaged in plastic pucks, and sold to the Leaf faithful for $50 a pop, adding $125,000 to MLSE's bottom line.

It's pocket change given that the company Peddie runs turns a net profit of more than $80 million annually, according to reports (as a private company MLSE doesn't release their financial records, and Peddie won't comment on them), but it adds up. Still, melted slush and bits of nylon mesh are nothing compared to irresistible synergies of Maple Leaf Square. "Toronto's first sports and entertainment condominium" will feature two towers, fifty and fifty-four floors respectively, rising in what were previously parking lots immediately west of the ACC. Leaf fans may be dreaming of Stanley Cups and the dim memory of horns honking on Yonge Street when their team wins even a single round of playoffs, but in the meantime, if you are looking for a hotel or a sports bar or a daycare centre, or perhaps a massive gift shop for Leafs, Raptors, Toronto FC and Marlies gear, you need look no further than Maple Leaf Square.

The area between the towers and the arena gives the development its name. It is a rare spot of public space where fans who aren't making a direct donation to the company by actually buying something with the famous blue and white logo on it can still feel a part of the action. There will be a massive outdoor television screen, and Peddie envisions a gathering place, a corporate hearth where the people can warm their Maple Leaf souls. "I was in New York the night of the presidential election," Peddie segues. "My wife and I were staying at the Trump and we walked down to Times Square and were there when Obama took Ohio. It was the place to be; my wife bought an Obama hat [non-licensed apparel alert!] off a street merchant," he says. It's a nice story, but pure Peddie, as he seamlessly connects the spontaneous outpouring that accompanied Barack Obama's historic election with some unrealized, though doubtless equally momentous moment in MLSE's future, maybe a return to the play-off for the Leafs or an MLS title for Toronto FC. "You want to be an entertainment centre, a destination," he says, getting back on message. "It's all about enterprise value. It's the metrics, but it's also the emotion around the brands."

And it was a good business deal too. The land, pur-chased in 2003, has doubled in value, Peddie figures. And the condos, all 872 of them, sold "like that," he says, snap-ping his fingers. Ninety-five percent had been claimed before a shovel even went in the ground, as buyers put their money down on everything from 400-square-foot studios selling for $197,000 to 2,100-square-foot penthouses fetching $1.3 million. Other features include a 48,000-square-foot underground grocery store and over 226,355 square feet of office space. They own 38 percent of the project (the rest is owned by Cadillac Fairview, the real estate arm of the Ontario Teachers' Pension Plan. "You get a bullet payment when you sell the condos. You make your profit there. Then it's a profit stream from running your hotel, the stores renting out the space . . . It's a nice little business."

❦

SAY WHAT YOU LIKE about Richard Peddie and his tenure with the Leafs, but don't try to make the case that the guy does not know business. When he took over the helm at MLSE, the job was a culmination of several themes for the then-forty-nine-year-old executive. He'd been marketing products for more than thirty years at that point.

He started in sales and marketing with Colgate-Palmolive in 1970 and moved to General Foods three years later as a brand manager. In 1983, Peddie became president of Hostess Snack Foods, a subsidiary of General Foods, and two years later he took over at Pillsbury. It was a career path that helped him get into the sports industry, but it didn't necessarily prepare him for it. "I'm at Pillsbury and we're having a really good year, but my brother is at Campbell's and they're having a really good year, too. But no one gets a parade and a trophy, even if we're kicking Del Monte's butt," he said. "Here, there is one parade and one trophy. It's much more Darwinian. You can finish second and we're losers. There, a customer might call a 1-800 number to complain; here, they're sitting behind you and booing."

He left the glamour of packaged goods for another iconic Canadian sports entity when he was tapped to run the SkyDome in 1989, just months after the building's historic opening. His success there was all the more remarkable given the snake pit of conflicting interests he was required to preside over. The organizational structure of SkyDome was such that the Blue Jays' two World Series wins and the flawless roof openings and closings and the 250 event-days each year that Peddie was able to book were like the brave face an outwardly accomplished family puts on for the neighbours. When no one was watching it was a roiling, hateful mess of infighting among the consortium which—along with the provincial and federal governments—paid nearly $600 million to build the landmark,

Peddie may have learned his upbeat "new-and-improved" shtick selling croissants and potato chips, but he perfected it at SkyDome. Not long into his term there he realized that the economics of the stadium wouldn't work. Its debt load and expenses simply outweighed revenues. At Peddie's suggestion the stadium was eventually put up for sale, fetching $151 million in 1994. "That sale involved two years of due diligence," he told *Toronto Life*. "For two years I kept saying to my staff: 'Just keep doing your job. We'll put in 250 events. Keep the place clean. Be friendly.'"

For his part, Peddie knew when to bolt. "We'd just come off a World Series," he was quoted as saying. "Three months later there was a baseball strike. The Jays were shitty. Attendance dropped. My timing was impeccable."

He spent two years as president of Labatt Communications, then the parent company of The Sports Network, Discovery Channel and Dome Productions. He also spent five months in 1993 running the Palestra Group, the bid company put together by Larry Tanenbaum that eventually finished second to the Bitove-Slaight group in their effort to bring an NBA franchise to Toronto.

Allan Slaight, one of Canada's most powerful broadcasting executives, became the majority owner of the Raptors when he triggered a buy-sell provision in his partnership agreement with John Bitove. And Richard Peddie would become the franchise's somewhat less unlikely first president. "Richard, you're the only guy in the country who has general manager, packaged goods and facility and broadcast experience," Slaight said. "Come run the Raptors for me."

Peddie got his chance to run an NBA team, however unlikely that might have been when he made it a personal goal back when he was an undergraduate scribbling in his journal in the late 1960s. How badly did he want the job, to be in the sports and entertainment business? "I'd probably be retired now if I'd stayed with Pillsbury and gone to the US and cashed in stock options at the right time," he says. "I was a 1 percent owner at NetStar [then the parent company of TSN, RDS, The Discovery Channel and Dome Productions], we were going to do an IPO and the day I walked away I knew I was walking away from $5 million. But I did it because I'd always dreamed of running a sports franchise, so how could I not? I love basketball. I love sports and concerts. I have no regrets. I live a dream. Sometimes a nightmare . . ."

IT'S HARD FOR ALL OF US not to pinch ourselves when we think of all the dreams Peddie has made a reality: the million-person database . . . the customer-relationship marketing . . . the cross-selling. So much we never knew we were missing, so much we will be reminiscing about for years.

But there is still Peddie's nightmare to account for. His money-making machine disguised as a hockey team has gone forty-two years without a visit to the Stanley Cup final, a quarter of those silent springs under his watch. And counting.

Could it be that the president of MLSE doesn't put the same careful planning into building a winning team that he does into making money? Peddie prides himself on knowing MLSE's financials inside and out. But ask Peddie how the Leafs' hockey development budget measures up against other NHL teams, and his answer is, "What do you mean by measurement?" For most teams it's not a huge expense. When scouts travel they aren't staying on Central Park South in New York—more like the Four Points by Sheraton in Kamloops. Logic suggests that the highest-revenue team in hockey, playing in a city that's mad for a Cup, would blow the rest of the league away when it came to spending on finding talent. The salary cap dictates that the Leafs can no longer outspend their rivals on player salaries, but they can spend all they like on scouts and coaches. If you want to improve, according to the Peddie mantra, you measure. But suddenly the numbers escape him. "I can't remember where we're at," he says. "But I look at it."

Do the Leafs spend more than any other hockey team?

"No," he admits. "We haven't to date."

But it is not so much what Peddie doesn't do that his critics blame for the Leafs' stumbles. It's what he can't seem to help himself from doing. If there is one word most associated with Richard Peddie, it is some version of "meddle." Punch "Peddie" and "meddle" into Google, and hundreds of references come up. In general they occur in passing, a way to explain away the hiring of the likes of John Ferguson Jr. as the Leafs' general manager, which began one of the most tepid and unfocussed eras in Leafs history. "Putting Ferguson in place, as awkward as it was, allowed Richard Peddie and the MLSE board to meddle and have their say on all the important hockey matters," wrote *Toronto Star* sports columnist Damien Cox in a blog post when the Leafs were poised to announce the hiring of Burke in November 2008. "It kept them in control after several years of having [Pat] Quinn report directly to Steve Stavro and no one else."

Or as *Globe and Mail* Leafs writer David Shoalts wrote in January 2006, after Peddie fired Toronto Raptors general manager Rob Babcock: "Peddie is a careerist who used his silky-smooth moves in the boardrooms to work his way up the business world and into MLSE through its basketball operations. He . . . was smart enough to limit his direct meddling in the sports operations to the Raptors. That changed with Ferguson's hiring." By all means, feel free to do your own Google search. The story is the same every time. Somehow, a marketing expert and potato-chip salesman inserted himself into a bitter power struggle between two of the most respected men in hockey: former Leafs president Ken Dryden and head coach Pat Quinn. Quinn was stepping down as GM, but insisted on playing some part in figuring out who would succeed him (in other words, he wanted to hire his new boss). Since the feuding Quinn and Dryden were never going to accept the guy the other wanted, Peddie's candidate got the nod. Enter John Ferguson.

And, eventually, exit Quinn. Shortly after he guided Canada to the gold medal at the 2009 World Junior Championships, Quinn explained how the wrong guy got the job: "My rights were in the contract to say that I and the president were supposed to make the hiring of the new general manager. Well, the president at the time was Ken. Ken had moved on and now Peddie was to be the new president of the hockey team as well, and I assumed that's what happened. I never knew that for a fact. All I know is in the process I was involved early on with the initiation of putting some candidates up to go through the process, and at the end of the day I was not the guy that made the selection with the president. So that was that."

"Meddle?" demands Richard Peddie. "Name an example? I've hired the guys. Maybe I've hired the wrong guys. But I've never changed a decision," he says. It might even be true. But then came January 22, 2008, and the introductory press conference for Cliff Fletcher, whom Peddie tapped to be the club's interim general manager following Ferguson's dismissal. For a few brief moments during Fletcher's opening remarks, Peddie's lips could be seen moving, mouthing the words as the Fletcher spoke them. The clip from the live press conference quickly become a YouTube classic and a handy bit of shorthand for Peddie's accusers. Scripting your GM's remarks looks a lot like meddling.

Peddie's heard it all before. He'll own up to a mistake hiring Ferguson—now that he's scrubbed that stain by hiring Brian Burke. "I had more hope for him," he says of Ferguson. "He'd done everything. Sat at the dinner table with his dad [longtime NHL player and executive John Ferguson Sr.]. Our due diligence on him was really good. He had the academic credentials. I really thought he was the prototypical [up-and-coming] general manager. I remember [Toronto Blue Jays president and chief executive officer] Paul Beeston told me the person should have really strong media skills and I discounted that. You really need that here."

Interesting. Many Leaf fans thought Ferguson's errors were things like mistaking Andrew Raycroft for a number-one goalie, or believing Bryan McCabe's impressive one-timer was enough to justify the kind of multi-year, multi-million-dollar contract usually reserved for defencemen who don't generally hand the puck over to opposing forecheckers at crucial moments. But no. Ferguson's problem was that he wasn't good with the media. God knows what Peddie would have made of Conn Smythe.

❦

IF THERE'S A MAN who's at once sympathetic and bemused by Peddie's low regard among the denizens of Leaf Nation, he occupies an office no more than a minute's walk north of the MLSE CEO's door, though miles away in terms of visibility and scrutiny. No one has ever left vitriolic voice mail on Tom Peddie's home phone. Why would they? He helps run a business. He doesn't tinker with someone's obsession. Like his older brother, Tom has enjoyed an exemplary career since graduating from the University of Windsor. The parallels are striking. Each of them started out with massive US-based packaged-goods conglomerates—Tom at Procter & Gamble while Richard was at Colgate-Palmolive; each ventured into the media industry and each has a top executive office with a lower Bay Street address. Tom's is at 181 Bay Street, BCE Place, where he's the chief financial officer for Corus Entertainment, the Canadian entertainment giant that includes YTV, Teletoon and Treehouse, fifty-two radio stations, and leading animated content creator Nelvana. And while helping run a media company that trades both on the TSX and the NYSE is pretty sexy for an accountant from Windsor, it's not running the Leafs. It's Tom who has news alerts about Richard sent to his desktop, not the other way around. "Would I want that job? No way," says Tom. "I wouldn't want to work those hours and be out to eighty games a year. That's not how I'd want to spend my evenings. It's not the dream job everyone thinks it is all the time."

Born a year apart—Richard, the older brother, was born January 31, 1947—they grew up "best friends" in Tom's words, in a modest three-bedroom, post-war home on a half-acre lot backing onto the Roseland Golf Course in south Windsor, about eight miles from downtown. As kids they were bound by common interests and mutual self-interest. When it came to baseball, Richard was the pitcher and Tom the catcher. Growing up, they were drawn more to basketball than hockey, playing in their driveway, taking in local high school and university games and making the occasional trip across the border to watch the Detroit Pistons. Summer evenings were easily whiled away by sneaking onto the golf course, which they did enough that they boasted single-digit handicaps. Tom was the better golfer, but one summer it was Richard that finally made it to the final round of the club championship. Tom caddied for him. "It went into extra holes," says Richard, chuckling. "And our backyard was next the eleventh fairway, maybe a 7-iron away. Tom had been warning me that I was standing too close to the ball on my practice swings, but I ignored him. Anyway, sure enough I'm in a playoff, take a practice swing and accidentally hit the ball and I lose, just like that [by incurring a penalty stroke]. My brother dropped the bag and walked into our yard." Family time was spent in the countryside, often at nearby Point Pelee, catching salamanders and identifying birds.

Rather than the sometimes-unhealthy rivalry that can mark brothers of relatively equal talents so close in age, Richard and Tom seemed to make each other better. "He's a great sounding board. We were in similar fields so we could bounce ideas off each other," says Tom. The brothers ran together; they were best men at each other's weddings—"Tom's done it twice," jokes Richard. He's a proud uncle to Tom's daughters, but says that he and his first wife, former *Toronto Sun* executive Trudy Eagan, were too career-oriented to have children. "Kids were never something Richard wanted to do," says Tom. Many of those talks came during the brothers' long and successful recreational running careers. A lot of the implied criticism of Peddie—or the idea of Peddie—stems from the notion that he's merely a marketing slickster who has interjected himself into a hockey operation that runs on passion and pride; the epitome of style over substance. What could this *business guy,* this *marketing guy* know about the blood and guts and pain and glory of sports? It's naive, of course. Business considerations have been primary in the NHL since Red Wings owner Bruce Norris lied to his players and swore them to secrecy to keep the salaries of the likes of Ted Lindsay, Gordie Howe and Alex Delvecchio artificially below market value. And it ignores the point that in Peddie's decade or more running two major-league sports teams he's probably only employed a dozen or so athletes as mentally tough as he was during a fifteen-year affair with marathon running, many of his training miles compiled alongside Tom. Peddie ran his first marathon in Ottawa in 1978, clocking 3:46. Five years later he ran his personal best of 2:46:03 at the Detroit Marathon. "It was thrilling. I remember coming down the chute the last 200 yards and being so high," he says. "I ran

2:46:03 . . . but to this day I say I ran 2:46. If I'd been focused I could have run 2:45:59 and I'd tell you I'd run 2:45. So now I think, fuck, I wasted those four seconds!" In 1988 he ran 2:48 at Boston at age 41. Sore knees have curtailed his running of late; "You'd have to time me with a calendar now," is his standard line. But he can rhyme off his training routine like he's got a race next week. "I'd run 65–75 miles a week, but I got up to 110 miles on big weeks," he says. "Intervals were Tuesdays or Thursdays, a five-kilometre time trial on Saturdays, long runs on Sunday." Think Peddie is some kind of egghead interloper in the world of athletics? Go to a track and try and beat his best: "I tell people to go to a track and run a 1:35 quarter," he says. "Now do it 106 times in a row without stopping. It's mind-boggling to me, but I was able to do it, though I weighed forty pounds less."

Peddie says running appealed to him because he could keep track of his progress in precise increments, day by day, week by week. It's a trait he comes by honestly. His father, Lee, was a skilled tradesman, crossing the border to Detroit to work at a small parts supplier. His specialty was making the tools that were used to make the machines used in burgeoning auto industry, setting a micrometer to a fraction of millimetre, grinding steel to the most precise specifications. "He made a good living." Lee Peddie died when his oldest son was only 21. "But he was blue collar. He went to work clean and came home dirty." It all lends some backstory to one of Peddie's pet sayings: "What is measured can be improved." No wonder conversations about the Leafs drift to metrics before line changes.

＊

PEDDIE MAY FEEL HIS MANDATE is both to make money and bring Toronto the Stanley Cup parade it has been waiting for since the days when hockey coaches wore fedoras and chomped on cigars. But the fact is, his day job is to accomplish only one of those noble feats.

Fans may scream: "The Leafs aren't a brand! They're a team! Like we played on when were kids! Like when we played ball hockey and I was Darryl Sittler and my brother was Lanny McDonald! Brands are for soap. Brands don't bleed, sweat, thrill or disappoint." But it is Richard Peddie's job to quietly disagree, and to make note to the board of the fact that the Leafs do bleed and occasionally disappoint (all right, more than occasionally) only makes them the best brand going. That's what drives Grandma to pick up a Maple Leafs pillowcase for little Billy (only $19.99 at The Bay).

And Peddie, says Claude Lamoureux, the recently retired former president and chief executive officer of the pension fund that controls the purse-strings at the ACC, wants to end the Leafs' four-plus decades of futility as much as the next fan. "Richard, I can tell you, wants to win more than me. He is there daily. He gets criticized.

He is the face. If there's a bad decision, he is the dummy who hired this coach and not the other one."

But it is one thing to be called a dummy by the guys talking about the Leafs over a couple beers, and quite another hear it from the people who sign your paycheque. Peddie answers to Teachers', which has a duty—a fiduciary duty—to maximize its return on investment. Breaking even doesn't come close to cutting it for the Leafs' president. As a Canadian equity investment, explains Lamoureux, Teachers' return on MLSE is compared to the performance of the TSX. And the message is clear: Beat the index, or else.

"If you invested in the TSX and you had $100 on January 1, and the TSX was at 8,000 and by the end of the year the TSX was 8,800, then somebody here who invests in these kinds of investments and his return is less than 10 percent, he's a bum. At 11 percent you're a hero. When you have a lot of money invested it's hard to get these numbers, but that's how we benchmark."

Peddie understands those marching orders to the letter. "We're a long-term hold [for Teachers'] but we have to earn that every year," he says. "Can they take their money and get a better return somewhere else? Where can they want to put their money for maximum return? As long as we're delivering it we'll be a long-term hold. If we don't, if we're under-performing, they could get a new management team in here to see if they can perform. If not, it's 'Let's get rid of it.'"

For a decade, Peddie has thrived quite happily under those conditions. They are the same rules that applied when he was selling toothpaste or potato chips. He can play that game with the best of them. Mistakes? He'll wear some. But for every John Ferguson Jr. or Paul Maurice there's been a Toronto FC or a Maple Leaf Square. As Peddie says, if his performance was based on what happened on the ice alone, well, his tenure might have been shorter, but it's not, and he knows it. And just in case, Peddie has been making retirement sounds since he hired Raptors president Bryan Colangelo in March of 2006, saying, "I hope I've hired my last general manager." Of course that was before he fired Ferguson and hired Brian Burke. The reality is he'll never be fired; he's too slick. He will be retired before it ever comes to that. He's building a house on Bob-lo Island, a marina resort community that sits at the mouth of the Detroit River near Amerstberg, Ontario. Windsor and Detroit families of Peddie's generation rode a steamship ferry to the island for picnics or visits to the amusement park that it was best known for. For Peddie it's a haven among Red Wing fans. That's how it's going to go down. Peddie will leave on his terms. How he will be viewed? That's less certain. The calls at home have stopped. But there's still that treacherous walk from his office to the ACC, all fifty feet of it. On busy days, or during a losing streak, he can always take the route through the underground parking garage. But once a marketer, always a marketer.

When he's not going to use his platinum-level tickets, he occasionally leaves his office and wanders into the arena and up to the 300 level. He'll look for a pair of fans—a couple on a date, or a father and son—dressed in Leafs garb. He'll ask them if they'd like to use his tickets for the night. The rewards, he says, are immediate: big gushing smiles and thank-yous. And often emails— "tremendous emails," he says—about the backstory of the lucky pair's visit. Maybe it was their first game, or a special birthday, or a celebration after an illness. It warms a marketer's heart.

"It makes it all worthwhile," Peddie says. "I just hope they tell a couple of friends that Richard's not an asshole."

THE LEAFS DO IT AGAIN

FEBRUARY 12, 1972: The Leafs allow Bernie Parent to escape to the World Hockey Association, a year before they trade his rights, along with a second-round pick, to the Philadelphia Flyers for a first-round pick (Bob Neely) and a player to be named later (Doug Favell). Parent, in the following two seasons, wins two Stanley Cups, two Conn Smythe trophies as playoff MVP and two Vezina trophies as the league's top goalie. The Leafs, meanwhile, see a rotating cast of undependables guard their twine over the same span, among them Favell, Dunc Wilson, Pierre Hamel, Gord McRae and Eddie Johnston.

JUNE 26, 1975: Leafs, after drafting Doug Jarvis twenty-fourth overall, trade the 20-year-old centreman to the Montreal Canadiens for Greg Hubick. Jarvis goes on to become a four-time Stanley Cup champ, the NHL ironman by playing 964 consecutive games from 1975 to 1987, and a winner of the Selke Trophy as top defensive forward in 1984, a year after Hubick, a 77-game NHL career in his rear-view, winds up his pro hockey run in the Swiss league.

MARCH 5, 2003: The Leafs trade Alyn McCauley, Brad Boyes and a first-round pick (which became Mark Stuart) to San Jose for Owen Nolan: Nolan is hurt and the move flops, and Boyes becomes the first player drafted by the Leafs to score 40 goals since Wendel Clark. Sadly, he does it for the St. Louis Blues.

Tie Domi makes a clean getaway after a career spent dealing elbows after the whistle and robbing Leafs fans of accomplishments worth cheering about.

Chapter Three
Life as a Leaf

"Being a Leaf is probably the easiest job in the world; mediocrity is rewarded with stardom."

— *Luigi Trentadue, Toronto*

WHEN A TEAM doesn't win a Stanley Cup for forty-two seasons and counting—when it doesn't even make the finals for forty-two seasons and counting—and when it misses the playoffs for a franchise-record fourth straight season, there's a case to be made that it's suffering from more than just bad luck. There's a case to be made that it's suffering from a malady, that it's host to an infection. Does it need a name? Let's call it Blue and White Disease.

The symptoms are two-fold. In some cases it shows up as a mild-to-severe swelling of the cranium, develops into a goofy, pinch-me-I'm-dreaming grin and finally morphs into a grand sense of entitlement. In its mildest forms, Blue and White Disease affects only a player's ability to backcheck or take a shorter shift. In its most severe cases, it can be fatal to a hockey player's career. It is spread by slaps on the back from strangers, a ready stream of adoring (and often attractive) fans, and family and friends eager to share the glow of your celebrity. Though it is possible to recover from this affliction, the patient will generally relapse if he hears the words "your money is no good here" at a bar, restaurant, golf course, or car dealership. In its final stages, the disease affects a player's sense of smell and leads to the impression that his shit simply does not stink.

But it's a pernicious virus. In some victims the symptoms are almost diametrically opposite, making it difficult to diagnose or treat. In some cases, the infected player will notice an alarming shrinking of the testicles, tremors in the hands, particularly when handling the puck anywhere near another team's net, and a generally downcast demeanour, often accompanied by a pale complexion and dark rings under the eyes. The media is often blamed for the spread of this strain of the disease, as the constant questions about a lack of aggressiveness on the road and extended scoring slumps can bring the symptoms on quickly and make them more likely to persist. In its final stages it includes booing at the ACC, catcalls from passing motorists and a mocking dismissiveness on talk radio. Though the disease can be treated with a trade to another market, ideally in the US sunbelt, full recovery is rare.

Ron Wilson doesn't need much to get rolling, conversationally. Well, it's not really a conversation. It's more of an in impromptu lecture. On the topic of Blue and White Disease, Wilson has pretty much appointed himself the chief medical officer of health. Whether by vaccination, quarantine or amputation, his mission since arriving in Toronto has been to restore the Leafs' collective ego to its proper proportions. One afternoon after practice last season, Wilson paused outside the Leafs' dressing room and allowed that as much as his first year in Toronto has been about finding who among his cast of suspect characters might actually still be with the team when it is something the city can be proud of, part of the job has been to inoculate his team against the risks of simply playing for the Leafs. "Blue and White Disease? I think some of the attention can go to people's heads and you have to make sure your team is grounded all the time," says Wilson. "It's kind of harsh to say, but the fans' opinions aren't exactly accurate."

Wilson knows of what he speaks. He played a total of sixty-four games for the Leafs over the course of three seasons beginning in 1977–78, part of an undistinguished playing career that amounted to 177 NHL games spread over seven seasons. But he's still remembered for his round helmet and his unusual pedigree—he was a product of NCAA hockey, which was noteworthy back then. He played in Europe. For all that, but only because he was also once a Leaf, he's remembered. It's not a burden to him, but he still finds it amusing to be stopped by exiled Leafs fans as he's walking past the White House on his way to the Verizon Center in Washington, or to see the double-takes the two or three days a week he takes the subway from his mid-Toronto home down to Union Station. "No one expects to see you on the subway," he says. "Everyone's kind of walking around with their head down and by the time they look up and recognize you, you're gone."

Normalizing the experience of playing hockey in Toronto is key to building a long-term program of success here. "With the scrutiny you get and the idolatry involved, you can lose your sense of priorities here in a hurry," he says. "We talk about it quite a bit . . . [we] keep reiterating over and over that it's about *winning* with the Toronto Maple Leafs."

His preferred technique to ward off Blue and White Disease in year one was the verbal blowtorch. Over the course of a losing season, he seemed to systematically call out his players, both individually and as a group, taking any opportunity to skewer, poke, prod and generally remind everyone listening that playing on a losing hockey team made you a losing hockey player, Maple Leafs sweater be damned. How about Dominic Moore? The feel-good story of the suburban Toronto kid who was in the midst of a breakout season in his first chance to play a heavy dose of NHL minutes? "We tend to get so carried away in Toronto with a guy having a decent year," Wilson sniffed at one point. "He's a . . . third-line player who's taken advantage of the extra ice time to get those points, that's it. Scoring points on a really bad team, that's really all it is." No surprise, then, when Moore was shipped off to Buffalo at the trade deadline. What about Vesa Toskala? You have to treat your starting goalie with some kind of respect, right? Nope. "I would have expected Vesa to have much better numbers at this point. He's been inconsistent at best," Wilson said in February 2009, not long before Toskala's season was cut short by multiple surgeries. "I want to see him practise harder. You can say you're saving something in practice for the games. But if you are failing in certain parts of your game, the only thing to do is practise harder."

Any perceived attempt by the media to baby his club or lower expectations was consistently swatted away with Wilson's own special brand of disdain. "We have a practice that a quality team in this league might have . . . and it is seen as a punishment," he said after putting his club through a long skate that the media tried to suggest was punishment for poor play. "All of a sudden, it's, 'Oh my God, they're being kicked in the ass.' And they're not. You guys ought to go and watch the top teams in our league practise. It drives me nuts. Good teams practise hard every single day, and [the media in Toronto] lowers the bar on everybody. Like the practice in Phoenix [on December 5, 2009] at eight o'clock in the morning. We skated for thirty-five minutes and it was like, 'Holy cow!'"

It's caustic. It's entertaining—from afar at least—and it's all part of creating a culture where the perks that come from playing in hockey's most forgiving and faithful market are earned. "You got this sense when I first came here that it was about wearing a hat with a different logo," Wilson says, his now half-empty can of Diet Coke tracing big circles in the air to match his oratorical flourishes. "That it was about selling yourself. But when the team wins and you're really successful, all of that other stuff will take care of itself. It's almost like if I can play in that Toronto market, I can set myself up for life. Well, you're already set up for life if you're playing in the NHL. You're making a ton of money if you're a good hockey player—you don't have to worry about all that stuff. Your focus should be on doing what you need to do to make yourself and your team better, and winning the Stanley Cup. It's going to take a while, but we're going be patient in the pursuit of that."

The challenges Wilson is facing are hardly new, but trying to create a team dynamic in a city that inherently wants to celebrate the Leaf of the Day isn't easily solved. "It wasn't as bad in the '60s when I played there, but it was there," says Pat Quinn, who patrolled the blue line for the Leafs in 1968–69 and 1969–70 at the start of his eight-year NHL career. "But there's no question that some athletes don't want to play with that scrutiny and they do perform better without having to face it, where they can get away after the game. That's not possible in Toronto. It's too bad, because there's nowhere better, there's great joy to be had here."

If only the city weren't a Petri dish teeming with the Blue and White virus. Quinn coached some good teams in seven seasons behind the Leafs bench, but he couldn't quite heal the patient. "It can get in the way of team unity and being a good team because there are some players who recognize that they can create their own niche with the crowd that has nothing to do with team success," says Quinn. "It's about the individual, and when the individual becomes more important than the team you can have a problem. Because it's only teams that win at the end of the day, and that might be one of the biggest problems that exists there now. Those that know that they have the special niche with the fans or perhaps the ownership or whatever, where their performance is directed toward that reward, not the reward of winning or anything else. . . . Yes that happens and it is a problem. You hope you can overcome it somehow. But it's one of the reasons why the really good teams we had didn't get right over the top during the six or seven years when I was there. They were capable, but they didn't have the team harmony to get through it."

What does Blue and White Disease look like on the ice?

"Guys who take stupid penalties, guys who fight when there's no reason to fight, just to attract the love of the crowd," says Quinn. "Guys who break out of the system, who run over here and over there. It looks good but they're doing squat. Or guys who hang off the net in that scoring position on a power play—they do nothing, but something happens and they get a goal. He looks like a hero but he's been screwing it up for a minute and half before that. Going offside, not head-manning the puck. There's lots of that."

THERE IS NOTHING that prepares you for it. You're grinding away in your hockey career, pulling yourself up each rung of the ladder. The toast of small-town Canada in junior. Riding the buses in the anonymity of the American Hockey League as a young pro. Waiting for a shot. Then you make the League, and while the money is good, playing in Nashville or St. Louis or Phoenix is a lesson in humility. You're a big shot at the arena on game nights, but on Thursday afternoon at ShopRite? Not so much.

But then you get traded, or you sign as a free agent. And overnight you're a Toronto Maple Leaf. In an instant, your life changes. No longer a hockey player, you're now a celebrity. No longer a just a third-line plugger, now you're a Toronto Maple Leaf plugging away on the third line, and thus a source of debate for talk radio, a potential interview subject for any of the dozen or so media outlets that show up dutifully at every practice, every game, every pre-game skate.

"You can watch it from the outside as a kid growing up or you can live it every day as a fan, but until you're in that fish bowl, you'll never understand how truly difficult at times it can be on you," says Nick Kypreos, a Toronto native who played his last two seasons with the Leafs after plying his trade in the likes of Hartford and Washington before winning a Stanley Cup with the New York Rangers in 1994. "I was mesmerized by playing here. As much as New York gave me a wonderful experience that I had hoped to bring to Toronto, it is a beast. It is a beast when you gather up all the outside influences of playing in this city, whether it's [four] major newspapers following you or [four] sports channels or whatever, dissecting your thoughts, your emotions, your play, your activity on and off the ice. It's different than anything else, including New York."

Not that the Leafs all want to complain about horrors of being adored all the time. Kyle Wellwood played three full seasons in Toronto and loved every minute of it. A fifth-round pick who somehow found himself on the first line early in his career as a Leaf, Wellwood's soft hands and talents as a playmaker were a welcome anomaly on a roster shy on talent. He was supposed to be the winger who could finally take advantage of the space created by skating with Mats

Sundin. This was a guy who was traded straight up for Jason Spezza in junior, and Toronto was eager to anoint a slick young passer and finisher of its own now that both OHL snipers were playing in the big league.

The trouble was, the only part of Spezza's game that Wellwood imitated convincingly was his aversion to backchecking. After three seasons of watching in frustration as Wellwood held on to the puck too long or tried ill-advised passes at the blue line, the club was all but telling the hockey world that Wellwood was fat, out of shape and too lazy to do anything about it, a reputation that was only enhanced when the team finally gave up on him. He was waived in 2008 and eventually picked up by the Vancouver Canucks. He required three tries to pass the club-mandated fitness test in training camp.

One might think that being drummed out of town and having your professionalism questioned along the way would taint just about anyone's outlook. One might think wrong. "Playing for the Leafs was the funnest time of my life so far," says Wellwood over the phone from Vancouver one afternoon in the winter of 2009. "Every day it was exciting to come to the rink. It was always exciting to put on that uniform on Saturday night. People came up to you every day and wanted to talk about your hockey game. Every day felt special. Everywhere you went—groceries, movies—there was a pretty good chance that someone would recognize you or want to talk to you. It was fun for me. If I was married or had a family it might not be as fun, but for me, a young guy in the big city, it was great."

Win or lose, Wellwood was out on Saturday night, hitting any number of downtown clubs where bouncers were than happy to whisk some Leafs and their friends past the velvet ropes and straight to the VIP areas. Muzik, Brant House, Century Room, name the exclusive club— even Leafs on a bad team were welcome there. "Saturday night was the best night," says Wellwood. "You'd play and, especially if you won, you'd go out and the minute you show up at the club you cut the line, get a table, get a few drinks. As a young kid it was a lot of fun, I definitely miss it. If Tie was bringing you out, you got a lot of attention, but it was nice. It was tough for the guys who were married or had a girlfriend. There's always someone who wants a cell-phone picture taken and next thing you know you're on someone's Facebook page and there's a girl kissing you on the cheek. You have to be careful. But if you wanted attention from the girls, you could defi-nitely get it. I just think it's fun for them to hang out with an NHL player in Toronto. And if they'd had a few drinks it was even more fun." That Wellwood could play three seasons in what is supposed to be one of the most demanding places for a hockey player to ply his trade, undergo three surgeries, miss the playoffs all three years and wind up unceremoniously waived, and still say it was the "funnest time of my life" makes a pretty strong case about the ancillary benefits of citizenship in Leafland.

A player with a conscience might feel differently. A player like Tom Fitzgerald, perhaps. A fourteen-year veteran and a 34-year-old father of three when he signed with the Leafs as a free agent in the summer of 2002, he wasn't coming to Toronto for the nightlife. He celebrated his two-year, $1.85-million deal "with a bucket of popcorn and a bag of Skittles" as he took his family to the movies. A son of a longshoreman from Boston, he had an idea what playing in Toronto might be like based on his own experience as life-long Red Sox fan. "My attitude toward the Red Sox, as a huge fan, is up and down like the weather. Wins and losses, I go up and down. This guy's great. The pitching stinks. We need a new catcher. We've got to fill this hole. And Leafs Nation was the same thing," says Fitzgerald. "I was a third-line player at best, a fourth-line guy for the Toronto Maple Leafs. And you'd go to the movies, you'd go to a hockey rink with your kid, and people are constantly recognizing you, asking for an autograph. 'Am I bothering you?' No, it was never a bother. But I remember saying at the time, 'I couldn't imagine being Mats Sundin walking around the city.'"

Pat Quinn had long coveted Fitzgerald, a scrappy, no-nonsense veteran who would fit in as a depth player on any team. But when they came calling in 1999 and tried to convince him to come north after some solid years playing for the Florida Panthers, Fitzgerald balked and ended up joining the expansion Nashville Predators. The money was the same; the scrutiny wasn't. "My first kick at free agency, it came down to Nashville and Toronto. At the time, I just felt I wasn't ready for that pressure. You put pressure on yourself as a player, but you fly under the radar a little bit when you're playing in South Florida. You go to Toronto, you'd better expect— *expect*—to be put under a microscope. I didn't feel like I was mature enough at the time to handle that pressure. At the time, I was scoring ten to fifteen goals a year. What if I scored four?"

But after four seasons in Nashville as team captain, Fitzgerald felt ready when the Leafs came calling again. This time Fitzgerald went for it, lured by the chance to join an Original Six team that had made it to the semi-finals the season before. Scrutiny? There was some, not always good. The Leafs lost in seven games to Philadelphia in the first round of the playoffs in 2002–03. "I had a buddy, after we lost to Philadelphia, he came to me after with a six-pack of eggs. He said, 'Do you want to throw 'em at your house or do you want me to?'

"Everyone had an opinion," says Fitzgerald, now the director of player development for the Pittsburgh Penguins. For the most part it was fun, or funny. The exception being when his kids would hear it from friends at school when their dad had a rough night, or when he had to give consideration to taking his name off his eight-year-old son's hockey jersey because people in the rink would see the Leaf player at the game, see the name on the jersey, put two and two together and turn a boy's hockey game into a referendum on the old man's talents. "I could care less if someone tells me I suck," says Fitzgerald. "When you're telling my kids, 'Your dad really sucks,' that's when it crosses the line. My wife was really sensitive to it, because your kids are being exposed to that part of the game."

The downside of celebrity in Toronto can be annoying at times, to say the least. If it isn't armchair powerplay quarterbacking, or overzealous enthusiasm, there is always the rumour mill. Remember the "Wendy" Clark rumours in the early '90s? The idea that the rugged Leafs captain was gay, and fond of figure skater Toller Cranston? Remember Vancouver fans maliciously chanting "*Wen*-dy, *Wen*-dy" when the Leafs faced the Canucks in the 1994 semi-finals? (Or coach Pat Burns shrugging off the rumours to reporters with the memorable quip that if being gay meant playing like Wendel Clark, then he wanted to be gay too?) If anyone needs to be reminded from time to time that that unfounded, salacious rumours pre-dated the Internet, surely the whispering about Number 17 should offer convincing proof.

(In any case, Toronto nightlife impresario Nick Di Dinato can put the rumour to rest. "We would go out, and if you have a few too many drinks your inhibitions go away and your true person comes out. And he was always chasing women. For sure. I knew that Wendel Clark was not even slightly that direction. Him and Todd Gill lived in a place on Madison Avenue and they had a backyard hot tub and you would go to parties there and it would be them, a few other Leafs, and a lot of girls in the hot tub.")

Still, no one ever died from a bit of celebrity gossip. In February of 1994, Doug Gilmour began getting threatening mail and disturbing phone calls from a female "admirer" complaining he wasn't being nice enough to her. The caller grew increasingly volatile and irate. "'I know where you live,' that kind of thing," says Gilmour. "And finally I got one that said, 'Next Thursday, after practice, you'll be dead.'"

He reported it to NHL security and the police, and it made for a day of high drama. The police took the threat seriously. Gilmour was given around-the-clock security. When the day came, the Gardens was surrounded by undercover officers, and Gilmour was given a police escort to and from practice, but nothing happened. The threats eventually stopped. Gilmour suspects they may have come from a disgruntled Gardens employee, but he's not sure. Now he has a lasting memory of the other side of being loved by Leafs Nation. "I was pretty shaken, especially when they tell you a date they're going to kill you," says Gilmour, who was coaching the Kingston Frontenacs of the Ontario Hockey League in 2008-09. "I was like, okaayyy. Do I have to practise that day?" The answer in Pat Burns' world: yes.

At the other extreme, celebrity Leafdom can be troubling for other reasons. Though they think of themselves as the most sophisticated fans in hockey, Leafs Nation can be just as clueless as the average Columbus Blue Jacket season-ticket holder. This was the city, after all, where Larry Murphy was essentially booed out of town for being Larry Murphy, a slow but unflappable puck-moving defenceman. He won two Stanley Cups as a regular in Pittsburgh before he got to Toronto and won two more as a regular in Detroit after he left Toronto. He won two Canada Cups and scored more than 60 points eleven times in his career. But as a Leaf he was a whipping boy—overpaid and too slow.

"What happens in Toronto is that fans have expectations of a player, and when they don't think the player is matching their expectations they begin to target him, and that's what happened to Larry," says Mike Murphy (no relation), who coached the Leafs between Pat Burns and Pat Quinn. "We never had a problem with how Larry was playing. He gave us what we asked for. But the fans—through the media and the broadcasters—targeted him. It got to the point where around the trade deadline I was sitting with Cliff [Fletcher] and said if there's a place to move Larry, we should do it for his sake."

More than a decade later, Larry Murphy still won't delve into his time playing for his hometown team, refusing several interview requests for this book. He entered the Hockey Hall of Fame in 2004, the first year he was eligible. "I don't know why it is," says Bob Stellick, principal of Stellick Marketing and Communications and previously director of business operations and communications for the Gardens, "but Leafs fans have a long history of ignoring talent."

And when they are not booing future Hall-of-Famers, they are showering goons and grinders with breathless adoration. To be truly loved in Toronto, a player must be able to score a goal from time to time (thought not too often) and fight often. Take Tiger Williams. Take Darcy Tucker. Even Wendel Clark seems to be remembered more for his talent with his fists than his superior wrist shot. But for a true study of what Leaf fans admire most, take the example of two of Toronto's most revered players of the last decade: Mats Sundin and Tie Domi.

The two of them played eleven seasons together in Toronto, both arriving for the 1994–95 campaign. Sundin scored 420 goals as a Leaf, was the stoic captain and led the club to the brink of the Stanley Cup finals twice. Domi scored 83 goals and punched a lot of people in the face, several of them on Sundin's behalf. (An arrangement Sundin didn't mind in the least. Leafs tradition calls for a new father to take his teammates out for dinner. On the occasion of the birth of his daughter, Domi decided to take the team to an upscale steakhouse called Morton's. His teammates showed no mercy, ordering only the most expensive items on the wine list and the menu. Estimates put the bill at $10,000, enough to make even Domi sweat. But the bill never came. Sundin had taken care of it. "That's why," said Domi, "nobody's going to lay a hand on that guy this season.") One of them was not only a clutch player, but unerringly gracious off the ice as well, while the other was by turns a clown and a bully whether he was wearing the blue and white or not. Leaf fans had a hard time deciding which one they liked better.

By almost any reasonable standard, Domi was a loud-mouthed, spotlight-craving boor. Scoring the series winner in overtime in game six of the second round of the 1996 playoffs at Mellon Arena in Pittsburgh was the biggest moment of Garry Valk's journeyman career. For the first time, he was object of attention in the Leafs' dressing room. And there was Domi, like a mean-spirited schoolboy, making silly faces over the circle of reporters that had formed around his teammate. "What are you talking to him for? What did he do?" Domi wasn't about to cede the spotlight without comment.

Like a Sean Avery or a Jarkko Ruutu, Domi could actually play hockey when he wasn't playing the buffoon on the ice. But he couldn't seem to help himself. In 1995 he received an eight-game suspension for knocking out Ulf Samuelsson (admittedly, not a very gentlemanly player himself) with a gloved sucker-punch. Asked why he had snapped, the Leafs enforcer answered that Samuelsson had called him a "dummy." As if to prove Samuelsson right, Domi ruined perhaps the best season of his career with an unwarranted and premeditated assault on New Jersey's Scott Niedermayer, one of the league's classiest players, in game six of the second round of the 2001 playoffs. For two days, instead of focusing on one of the most important games in franchise history, Toronto was in a tizzy over Tie and his suspension. Somehow, the guy with perhaps the least to contribute on the ice was the off-ice focus. Whether or not the media circus that followed in the wake of Domi's cheap shot was a distraction in the dressing room, the Leafs surrendered to a fired-up Devils team on the road in game seven.

In contrast to the volatile Domi, Sundin never seemed to sweat. Beat reporters assigned to the team can remember only one occasion when Number 13 ever lost his cool. That memorable moment came when some sportswriters overheard Leafs assistant coach Mike Kitchen asking Sundin about a story that he was going to get engaged to long-time girlfriend Tina Fagerstrom (she didn't make the cut in the end). When he learned the topic had found its way into the newspapers, Sundin invited reporters to mess with his privacy at their peril. The next day he stood in front of the small scrum (the Leafs were on the road, otherwise it would have been a large scrum), and said simply, but angrily, to the assembled journalists: "You fuckers."

Domi's love life, in contrast, always seemed available for public consumption. Guard his privacy? Try to find a Toronto burger or pizza or souvlaki joint that isn't decorated with a signed Tie Domi glossy. His dating of B-actress Tia Carrere coincided with his first separation from his wife, Leanne. (His teammates dropped the "e" and added an "a" to the nameplate over his stall.) His divorce came about when he was linked with former Conservative MP and auto parts heiress Belinda Stronach. The ugly domestic split was front-page news.

In some other cities, perhaps Domi's transparent attention-seeking would make him a source of amusement or even sympathy. Not in Toronto. Keep in mind that the reason the Leafs invented their mascot, Carlton the Bear, was in part that they were having an increasingly difficult time securing players for personal appearances. Domi almost put the poor bear out of work. He was a one-man personal-appearance machine, willing to be present, photographed, auctioned off, whatever. In the end, maybe Leaf fans just want to be loved. Domi trailed Sundin by 337 goals over the course of their careers in Toronto. But in jersey sales? They were neck and neck.

CALL IT IRONIC. In a city that loves its hockey team above all else, where the Leafs are supported regardless of their performance, there's a case to be made that the unconditional love is part of the problem. Like pushy stage parents or insecure lovers, Leaf fans seem to want something so badly they end up scaring it away.

But it doesn't have to be that way. Sometimes it's not the city infecting the Leafs; sometimes the Leafs infect the fans. In that case the condition is not Blue and White Disease. It's called Playoff Fever, and it is not unpleasant at all. Perhaps the most beloved teams of the post-'60s era, the Gilmour and Clark teams of the early '90s, seemed to find a way to thrive in Toronto, feeding off the passion they created.

The team's stars certainly didn't shy away from the public eye. "A guy like Doug was a rock star in the early '90s here. A *rock star*," says Nick Kypreos. "And Wendel too. But he always seemed to control the doses that he wanted as opposed to having that energy control him. And that's a big difference. At the end of the day, he never let it affect his play on the ice. Some guys get the pecking order confused, and Doug was the type of guy who understood that as long as he played at a high level, everything else will follow."

Those memorable teams seem shrouded in a haze of nostalgia now. The Leafs that Wendel Clark captained to consecutive semifinal appearances played in a barn that has now been all but forgotten, in a different conference and a division that many fans today have never even known was called the Norris. But there is perhaps no greater symbol of the passage of time than the bar just down the street from the gloomy quiet of Maple Leaf Gardens, at 72 Carlton Street. For nearly fifteen years the low-slung two-story building was home to P.M. Toronto, otherwise known as "the watering hole of the gods." Opened in 1986—Wendel Clark's rookie year—it quickly became the favoured hangout for the Leafs and one of the hottest bars in Toronto. It was where Doug Gilmour, the Leafs leading man, used to squire teenaged Amy Cable, the prettiest of the Gardens usherettes and the future (and now former) Amy Gilmour. It was where the Leafs could walk in the front door and be treated like conquering heroes, and then slip into a private room in the basement where the bottomless supply of beer was on Molson's tab.

Owner Nick Di Dinato's relationship with the players started gradually and without any real intent. He had a bar, it was close to the rink, there was a dance floor, there were girls: Dave Ellett, come on down! As the Leafs started showing up more regularly, Di Dinato realized he needed to create their own space for them—having pseudo tough guys wanting to challenge Wendel Clark after a few beers was not going to work in the long term (or in the very short term for anyone on the business end of a Clark right cross). The basement room was set up in short order. It was hardly palatial: bench seating around the perimeter of the 700-square-foot room; a bar, a pool table, a steel door without a window, and someone manning it. "No one knew it was there other than the Leafs. It was in the back area, downstairs. By the washroom there was another door that led to this dark hallway with the paint peeling to a set of stairs at the back," say Di Dinato. "People would be like, 'Where are you taking me?'"

Just a bunch of regular guys throwing back cold ones after a hockey game, with fetching lasses ready to make their way to the inner sanctum if summoned. "It was their space," says Di Dinato, now the president and chief executive officer of the Liberty Entertainment Group, but then a first-time restaurateur, a twenty-something kid from Little Italy rubbing shoulders with his heroes.

"They could come to the restaurant and invite the people they wanted to—usherettes or whoever—but it had to be specifically who the players wanted. Wendel had a key to the room. . . . They were young guys at the time and it was like having their own house party." By the time Doug Gilmour arrived from Calgary and the 1992–93 Leafs began to take off, the routines were well established: play at home on Saturday night, head to P.M. Toronto, repeat. It got the point where they were having team meetings in their off-site, brewery-sponsored clubhouse. Did it contribute to the club's success? "For sure, a hundred percent," says Gilmour.

The fifteen years since his shining Leafs moments have treated Gilmour well. The mullet is gone, as is the emaciated playoff look and the toothless grin. He's not exactly paunchy, but he looks well fed. At forty-six years old there's not a hint of grey, but that could because he's taken a few two-minute penalties for looking so good.

The teeth are white and straight, the scars visible but nicely healed. He's moved on. His Toronto home sold, his divorce from Amy final. But he can recall those Leaf years without much effort.

"It was a very tight-knit group, on and off the ice, and it definitely made us better," he says. "Everyone was excited for everyone else, no one was jealous." They did their share of bonding on the road, but at home too. Most of the younger players lived downtown and did nearly everything as a group. Saturday nights were team nights at P.M. Toronto. "It was a nice, local spot and they took care of us," says Gilmour. "We'd play at eight and by the time we were done it was 11:00 or 11:30, so it was nearby and we could all go. We had a lot of veteran leaders who made sure everyone was on the same program. It was a lot of fun."

Too much fun? Apparently not. As legendary baseball manger Casey Stengel observed about professional athletes and their nocturnal habits: "The trouble is not that players have sex the night before a game. It's that they stay out all night looking for it." Not a problem for the Leafs on a Saturday night at their clubhouse. "There was a slew of women. If they were into women, they could have their women. Most of the women were there to meet a hockey player," says Di Dinato. "That happened all the time. We had regulars there just to meet a hockey player. Some got to meet their hockey player, some didn't." In any case, according to the person who should know, their performance never suffered. "They had their fun," says Pat Burns, "but when it came time to play they were ready."

Need proof that times change? When the Leafs moved to the ACC, P.M. Toronto died. The Di Dinatos sold the business and gave up their lease. The Leafs' former rec room became Zippers, where a rainbow flag proudly flutters above the awning and the sign features a handsome, swarthy man wearing a white T-shirt and faded blue jeans, looking shyly down at his crotch. There's no Leafs memorabilia inside, just a plaque declaring it Toronto's best piano bar as recognized by the readers of *Xtra* magazine, Toronto's gay entertainment weekly. They don't line up to watch the hockey game on the big screens anymore on Saturday nights, nor hope to catch a glimpse of one of their heroes after the game. Nope. Saturday nights are for "Hard," featuring DJ Cory Activate ("You love when he gives it to you hard"), who pumps up the crowd in the name of male bonding of an entirely different sort.

For an aspiring restaurant and night club owner, dealing with the Leafs early in his career was a lesson in managing celebrity that has helped him cater to the likes of Brad Pitt and John Malkovich when the Hollywood A-listers are in town for the Toronto International Film Festival, or even the likes of Ian White and Matt Stajan today. "Whenever we have [the Leafs] in our venues we take care of them and control the environment for them.

They would never stand in line at one of our places. It wouldn't reflect well on us. We're in the city of Toronto, they're celebrities, they need to be treated that way," he says. The guy who once helped quarantine the Leafs from the dreaded Blue and White epidemic now seems to be spreading it.

Maybe replicating the kind of team Clark and Gilmour led so memorably back when the Leafs were more of a fraternity than a corporation is more difficult now that all the players are millionaires and many are brands in their own right. Bigger money begat richer tastes. The $5 pitcher has been traded for the wine list. There is more choice, with the sprawling and varied nightclub district beckoning, something that was in its infancy fifteen years ago. Beer and wings with the guys after the game? How about dinner at Harbour 60, the opulent steak house opposite the ACC, the closest thing the Leafs have to a hangout these days. The lighting is dark; the four-inch-thick well-marbled slabs of beef are displayed like art under glass in front of the open kitchen and the high-backed chairs are suitable for a king, as long as you have the credit card that can carry the ransom. "It's not how it was, put it that way. Does that have an impact on players and winning?" says Gilmour. "I don't know, but it's a good question."

THE LEAFS DO IT AGAIN

JUNE 14, 1978: The Leafs trade Randy Carlyle and George Ferguson to the Pittsburgh Penguins for Dave Burrows. Ferguson arrives in Pittsburgh in time to reel off four consecutive 20-plus-goal seasons. Carlyle, twenty-one at the time, goes on to play in four All-Star Games and win the 1981 Norris Trophy as the league's best defenceman, the year Burrows, himself an All-Star, retires.

AUGUST 1978: In an attempt to cash in on the bad publicity the club was receiving after owner Harold Ballard's decision to dismantle and incinerate the Maple Leaf Gardens gondola, Foster Hewitt's legendary broadcast perch, Ballard has Hewitt's name painted on the back of a pile of random chairs and attempts to sell them as though they were used by Hewitt.

MARCH 13, 2001: Leafs trade Adam Mair and a second-round draft pick that becomes Mike Cammalleri to the L.A. Kings for Aki Berg.

Left: Premier of Ontario, Dalton McGuinty. Right: Prime Minister of Canada, Stephen Harper. Centre: The man who would be king, Larry Tanenbaum.

Chapter Four

Find Hope in Larry Tanenbaum

"Think of all the coaches and general managers this team has had since 1967. Do you really think the problem is the coach or general manager? The problem has always been the ownership. Too bad owners can't be fired."

—Sam Brunetti, Toronto

IF A BAR CAN'T SAVE the Toronto Maple Leafs, can a Great Man? Is the team just a charismatic leader away from becoming the kind of organization that everyone who has ever worn a Leafs toque desires, nay, deserves? Is Larry Tanenbaum, whose only brush with championship hockey came as a wide-eyed student manager at Cornell University, a Great Hockey Man? Maple Leaf fans should hope so.

As long as the Ontario Teachers' Pension Plan maintains majority ownership of the colossus that is Maple Leaf Sports and Entertainment, it will always be for sale. That's just part of life as an asset. Nothing personal—even though the organization's wealth is tied to the personal passion of those who follow its teams and buy their branded merchandise. "Everything is for sale here," Claude Lamoureux, former president and chief executive officer of Teachers', is fond of saying, with his trademark cackle. "You like this table? I will sell you this table, for the right price." But Larry Tanenbaum is different. His investment in the team is personal.

"Larry goes to bed at night thinking about what needs to be done to make the Leafs winners," said a close associate. Tanenbaum describes himself as a "superfan." And while Teachers' can defend its relative lack of hands-on involvement as a good thing, citing the fact that the most important hockey franchise on the planet represents less than 2 percent of its estimated $88 billion worth of the fund's portfolio, Tanenbaum can't be so dispassionate, even if he wanted to be. He's got $250 million, or a quarter of his net worth, bet on blue and white. (In 2008, *Canadian Business* pegged his net worth at $950 million, or fifty-third on their annual list of wealthiest Canadians.) And unlike his most corporate of corporate partners, he is determined to stick around. "I will tell you this," Tanenbaum revealed in what has of late been an increasingly rare interview. "I will give it a fifteen-year time frame. By then I'll be seventy-eight years old. And if I haven't achieved what I should have achieved during that time frame, then it's time to get out."

"He's got hundreds of millions of dollars of his own money into this," explains a source close to the closest thing the Leafs have to an owner, "but he's got a lot of patience. That's what's really stood him well in his years in business. And if God gives him the strength, he's going to outlast Teachers'. He's going to put himself in position to call the shots." So, Leaf fans, you're stuck with him, basically. But this could be good.

Before the cynicism rises—and it's natural to question how the guy who signed off on John Ferguson Jr. and pushed for one last contract for Tie Domi could be the right man to run the whole shebang—give it some thought. Consider: Does ownership matter? Does having a primary, individual owner matter?

Entire organizations and eras can be reduced to a well-known shorthand. Historically, the NHL was shaped by big, bold owners, though not always for the best. And even today, when sports franchises have become corporations complete with mission statements other than, you know, "Just win, baby!"—which seems like the only one you'd need—people and personalities matter. The first generation of Red Wings Cup winners? Yzerman. The next? Lidstrom. The Red Wings way? Long-time owner Mike Ilitch. The first Canadiens five-Cup dynasty? Beliveau. The second? Lafleur. Islanders: Potvin. Oilers: Gretzky. And so it goes. Players, owners, coaches: there are countless examples of one person reversing the fortunes of a franchise through their gifts and willfulness. They can't do it alone, but their presence can set a tone that lifts those around them. Alexander the Great did some good work in Asia, after all, and Alexander Ovechkin has turned Washington, D.C., into a hockey hotbed almost single-handedly.

If you want to look for a root cause for the Leafs' flailings and failings since, oh, about 1967, think about it this way: When have they ever had that single galvanizing personality that could draw others to them by their will and vision, on or off the ice? Ballard? He was pretty much the opposite of that, as we've seen. Mean, small-minded, petty, cheap and vindictive. A great quote, but otherwise a disaster, and his team was largely a reflection of him.

Steve Stavro? There was some potential there. He loved being the Leafs' owner. It was deeply important to him. "He probably loved the Leafs as much as anyone possibly could," said former Leafs coach and Stavro favourite Pat Quinn. "The organization, what it stood for and what he wanted it to become."

There is no more treasured period in recent Leafs history than the magic springs of 1993 and 1994. Who will ever forget Nikolai Borschevsky's overtime winner in game seven against Detroit after the Red Wings had spanked the Leafs in the first two games of the series? Or the endless goaltending duels between Felix Potvin and St. Louis's Curtis Joseph, which came to an end when Wendel Clark rang a slapshot off Joseph's mask and opened the floodgates? Was the Leafs' resurgence simply what you would expect at the conclusion of the Ballard years and the arrival of a guy like Stavro?

Part of being an owner is connecting with your staff. Doug Gilmour tells a story of Stavro, shortly after he purchased his controlling interest in Maple Leaf Gardens Ltd. in early April 1994, making a visit to the dressing room at the Gardens before a game against the Winnipeg Jets on a rare Sunday night start. Insisting the players celebrate the occasion, he had them all drink a shot of the Macedonian equivalent of ouzo on their way out to the ice. "You knew it was his team," says Gilmour. "It was a little unusual, but we had a hell of a first period." In fact, they won 7–0.

While Stavro was never as prominent a public figure as either Smythe or Ballard (one wag dubbed him the Gardens Garbo for his aversion to talking to the press), he was no shrinking violet. Prone to table-thumping fits of temper and obsessively interested in the most minute aspects of the operation—it wasn't unusual for him to spend time in board meetings talking about the hot dog buns—his partners were there to provide money and perhaps an opinion, but otherwise stand back. "There was no doubt that Steve owned this place," said James Leech, who took over from Lamoureux as Teachers' president and CEO in September 2007, in an earlier interview. "And if he wanted someone hired, he'd go right to contract with the person. . . . That's not to be critical of Steve. He controlled 51 percent, that's the way it was set up."

And it worked. "In my experience, he was totally backing of the operations people and the players, one hundred percent," says Pat Quinn. "He was a guy that took great pride in being around that organization. He was not only supportive economically when we had to come up with money we needed, he'd go to bat for us with the board. But also emotionally, he was a guy that was there during the ups and downs. He was like a rock. Never a second-guesser, completely supportive. Really liked the players, but wasn't a guy who became a jocksniffer. There was a hierarchy as far as he was concerned. He knew the lines. He was a very experienced sports person. He'd been around it all his life—soccer and horse racing mostly—but he had a good feel for hockey as well. He was there to support our best efforts, he was ideal."

The most telling moment for Quinn came after the Leafs lost to the New Jersey Devils in game seven in the second round in 2001, blown out 5–1 at the Meadowlands. The Leafs had swept the Senators in the first round, won the opener against Jersey on the road, then dropped two games in overtime before taking a 3-2 lead in the series. Then they failed to close the Devils out on home ice in the infamous game six loss in which Tie Domi cold-cocked Scott Niedermayer in the dying moments. Having come so far and played so well, the Leafs flopped in game seven, managing only six shots on goal all night.

"It was one of the worst hockey games I've ever had a team of mine play," said Quinn. "I felt terrible—to not have your team show up—I don't know what happened to this day, but from the goal on out, we were no-shows.

"But I remember Mr. Stavro coming in. It was in the bowels of the building in New Jersey, and he came in, he was quiet, he sat down with the coaching staff. We just sat there for a little bit and he reached over, touched my shoulder and he said 'He makes the decisions.' *He* being the big guy upstairs, and he pointed up there. I don't know if it made me feel a whole lot better. But this guy understood that you can work your bag off, yet when the trial comes, sometimes you're not there for it, you're not up for it.

"He was hurting as much or more than we were. Nothing could have fulfilled his life like a Stanley Cup for Toronto and for the Leafs. That would have been a crowning thing for him. I still think about that today. I didn't know him a long time, but the time I knew him, he was a very impressive guy."

But Stavro was missing an essential quality to join that particular sub-species of Great Man known as Great Owner: deep pockets. He was losing money in the grocery business. Hemorrhaging it, actually. The Knob Hill Farms empire he built from a single grocery store in east-end Toronto was shut down in August 2000, closing ten stores and laying off 800 employees. Well before that, the Leafs very quickly went from profitable hobby to a line of credit for his other businesses. The grocery operation began withering, analysts said, in part because Stavro began diverting time and money to his hockey business. Now it was time for the Leafs to wither, as Stavro's time and money started to flow the other way.

Almost as soon as the club tasted success under Pat Burns and Cliff Fletcher in 1992–93, it came time to cut costs. Not two years after assuming a controlling role of his treasured club, Stavro's money problems resulted in a budget-related gutting of their roster. "It was pretty simple. Steve Stavro was putting pressure on Cliff Fletcher to cut payroll," recalls Detroit Red Wings executive Jim Devellano. Stavro's misfortune turned out to be Detroit's good luck. "[Larry] Murphy was their highest-paid player. Cliff called Scotty Bowman, actually, and asked if we had any interest." They did, and Murphy went on to quarterback the Wings' breakout and add two more Stanley Cup rings to his collection.

Stavro's money problems created an opportunity for Tanenbaum, who bought into the Leafs in 1996 for $21 million. The influx of cash helped the team regain their feet under Pat Quinn in the late '90s and helped pave the way for the creation of MLSE in 1998. So if Leafs fans are looking for someone to thank for six years in the playoffs and two trips to the conference finals between 1998 and 2004, they could start with Tanenbaum. Unfortunately, the story doesn't end there, which can be a problem for fans and players alike. "In a perfect world, I know players like to work for an [Mike] Ilitch or a [Tom] Hicks, where they know who they're playing for," said former Leaf and Sportsnet broadcaster Nick Kypreos of the owners in Detroit and Dallas, respectively. "That's one of the biggest problems [in Toronto]. There really doesn't seem to be any accountability from above. The players are held accountable by the coaches, and the coaches are held accountable by the general manager, and the general manager is accountable to the board of directors, but that's when everything else fall apart.... Who's in charge of the pension fund? Who's in charge of Maple Leaf Sports and Entertainment? That guy gets to walk around the city scot-free and that hurts the process of winning."

The question now is: Is Tanenbaum the guy to change that culture?

Who is Larry Tanenbaum, and why should any Leaf fan feel encouraged by his presence? Most days he can be found in his L-shaped office on the twenty-seventh floor of Scotia Plaza, a ten-minute walk from the ACC, but light years away in sensibility. His seats in the directors' section are six rows back from the bench, well within earshot of Ron Wilson's curses, but he gets his work done from the offices of Kilmer Van Nostrand, a merchant bank with investments in everything from the World Fishing Network to Boardwalk and Gaming and Entertainment, proprietor of a chain of charity bingos. Kilmer Van Nostrand was a family-owned construction business that had fallen on hard times when Max Tanenbaum—a Polish émigré who built a fortune in construction and real estate (hence former Leafs executive and current AM 640 host Bill Watters's summation of Tanenbaum as a PhD—Papa had Dough) bought it in the early '60s. Larry worked there, chipping in on road crews during his summers in high school and at Cornell. When he graduated with a degree in economics, he retired his work boots and assumed control of the company, eventually taking it global and merging in July 2000 with multinational construction materials company Lafarge North America in a deal worth $425 million. As one of the new company's largest individual shareholders, Tanenbaum served on the board of Lafarge until it was purchased by its French-based parent Lafarge SA in 2006, at which point Tanenbaum was able to sell his holdings for $233 million (US). It's not clear whether Tanenbaum would be able to beat Conn Smythe in the alley, but he would certainly be able to tangle with him in the world of business.

Having sold his construction company, Tanenbaum started Kilmer Capital Partners, then a $115-million private equity fund, moving his base of operations from a spot adjacent to a gravel pit in Downsview (a largely industrial and commercial area on the northwest border of Toronto) to the heart of the financial district. In his new Scotia Plaza offices, the lighting, the décor, everything reeks of sophistication and wealth. Arrive for a meeting, and a waiter (butler?) in black and white will materialize, produce a neatly folded linen napkin and inquire whether you'd like something to drink.

The whole experience is meant to communicate that you're in good hands here—and it does so quite convincingly. Tanenbaum knows what he's doing. "If I had a business problem or a community problem, he'd be the first guy I'd go to," says Gerry Schwartz, chairman and chief executive officer of Onex Corporation and one of the country's more noticeable deal-makers. "He always does his homework. He's always prepared and comes to a meeting chock full of good advice."

Being wealthy and smart and pals with Canada's business elite doesn't qualify Tanenbaum to be the man to lead the Leafs to respectability. It's not *that* easy. But this just might: After nearly fifteen years of being on the inside of the sports business, he knows that sports is not like his other businesses. "He's had to learn that absolutely, no question about it. This does not conform to the other rules of business, not one iota," says a source close to the MLSE chairman.

It's interesting, when you think about it. Perhaps the most basic expectation in sports is that players and teams will incrementally get better, at least until age or injury or something like Blue and White Disease begin to make them incrementally worse. But ownership—

at least as important as any individual player—is looked on as kind of static. But what if they have the capacity to improve just like, say, Luke Schenn does? "As an owner, you learn through experience, and if you're self-reflective and analytic you learn from what works and what doesn't," says Ted Leonsis, the majority owner of the Washington Capitals. Leonsis has built the Capitals into deep playoff contenders twice in this decade, and can go to bed at night with the kind of warm feeling any hockey fan would have knowing that young stars like Alex Ovechkin, Mike Green, Alex Semin and Nicklas Backstrom are on the roster.

Now Tanenbaum seems to have come to some of the same conclusions as Leonsis. "He knows it better now. You can't snap your fingers," says a Tanenbaum associate. "There's a science, naturally, but then there's an art of shaping it and building it, and an element of luck."

It's a departure from his outlook even half a decade ago. After quietly campaigning for the role of chairman following the reorganization of the ownership group finalized in February 2003, it almost seemed like Tanenbaum saw the ultimate success in hockey as merely another item on a to-do list. In a profile for *ROB Magazine* in March 2004, Tanenbaum pledged that the Leafs' Stanley Cup drought would end within the five-year term he was guaranteed as chairman. "I have at least five years and after that it's at the pleasure of the board, and at my pleasure," he said at the time. "And my pleasure is only if we have something tangible here, a Stanley Cup."

That self-imposed term ended in February 2008, with the Leafs as far as they've ever been from being serious Cup contenders. But Tanenbaum hasn't given any hint that he's actually going to step down. Nor does the board have any intention of asking him to, as is their right. Seriously, does anyone at Teachers' want to invite players and their families over to their houses? Tanenbaum does. Everything from contract negotiations to simple dinners (well, simple for his chef, anyway) to team parties have been held at Tanenbaum's elegant Frybrook Road estate.

Being hands-on and generous with time and perks is a requirement of ownership, many feel. As franchises get bigger and more corporate, providing a human face for the working class is an important consideration, and Tanenbaum has been willing to do that with his players over the years, and he clearly enjoys the role. When Burke was hired, it was Tanenbaum who took the front-row seat beside his wife, Jennifer, at the press conference, making sure she was tended to while her husband made like a groom at a wedding, attending a reception line's worth of interview requests. Over the years, there have been indications Tanenbaum may enjoy it too much, and perhaps that players may enjoy his patronage a little too much as well. On the basketball side, it's widely thought that his willingness to accommodate Vince

Carter contributed to team jealousies and turned the Raptors' star player into a coddled prima donna. On the hockey side, stories of Tie Domi flashing emails from Tanenbaum on his BlackBerry—to say nothing of Domi's trips to Tanenbaum's Lake Simcoe getaway—helped poison the dressing room and may have undermined Quinn late in his tenure with the Leafs. "I wasn't aware [of that stuff] at the time," Quinn says in an interview from his home in Vancouver. "But that certainly can become an issue. And it becomes an issue when a player uses it himself as leverage against his teammates or against a coach or a manager. . . . The top can undermine the people who are supposed to do the next jobs down, easily, by interfering in a sense, with the tools they need to have to be able run your part of the job properly. . . . It was only after I was let go that I heard that stuff, but if that's the case, shame on the players and shame on the others involved, because all it does is damage your organization."

All right, so Tanenbaum may not have been the solution to all the Leafs' problems so far. But after spending nearly a decade trying to get his arms around the mysterious elephant that is winning in professional sports, perhaps he has learned his limitations. He has come to realize that making bold predictions about winning a Stanley Cup on a schedule—or even a Major League Soccer Cup—is not worth the distraction. Media-shy at the best of times, Tanenbaum has gone a bit Garbo lately himself. Those closest to him can see a change in his outlook, says a source. "He knows that was a mistake on his part: saying that we would win a Stanley Cup here in five years was stupid. . . . It was absolutely heartfelt but, tactically, it was stupid. A Cup is the ultimate vision, but it will be when [they] bloody well earn it, deserve and build for it and do all the things necessary to win a Cup. There's no recipe for it. He knows that now. You can't open up a book and say 'Aha, that's how you win a Cup.'"

It may well be that, as a "superfan," Tanenbaum is no different from any other supporter of the blue and white. Maybe he just wants it all too much. He is still, at heart, a Jewish kid who grew up in WASP-run Toronto in the 1950s. The Leafs are in many ways a symbol of something that was unattainable a few decades before. "I'm proud of it as a Canadian and I'm proud of it as a Jew," Tanenbaum told *ROB Magazine*. He was raised in a kosher home, is prominently involved in a number of Jewish-oriented charities and won't attend games on Friday nights. "I'm just proud to be where I am. Does it give me satisfaction? Absolutely. Could this have been anticipated when I was in high school in 1955? Are you kidding? Not even close. It was legendary that Conn Smythe was not the most open-minded individual, and one would say a virulent anti-Semite. I didn't know him, but just the stories that come out." The irony of a Jew leading Smythe's team back to glory is not lost on the closest thing the Leafs have to an owner.

Tanenbaum is different too in that he doesn't quite fit the owner mould, which casts the guy who signs the cheques as a swashbuckling mogul. Beginning with the club's patriarch, Conn Smythe, owners of the Toronto Maple Leafs have tended to conform to the big-daddy stereotype that you might expect from those who like to make their money so publicly. It was Smythe, a veteran of two World Wars, who once showed up at Boston Garden in a top hat and tails after Bruins owner Art Ross accused him of having no class. He sent a thorny arrangement of roses to Ross with a note in Latin that said, basically, 'Stick 'em up your ass.' Which was fine until Ross handed them to his Latin-versed wife. But Smythe ran a first-class hockey operation and built a dynasty during his tenure.

That's the kind of role Tanenbaum would love to have: the owner who has the respect of the guys in the trenches but is able to manage the boardroom too. In the current system, however, Tanenbaum has a figure-head role that frustrates him at times, those close to him say. Here he is with a considerable amount of his own money on the table, but forced to watch as the shots are called by the likes of Peddie, a salaried employee who, for the most part, does the bidding of Teachers', which rotates its executives on and off the MLSE board. None of them have their own money invested in the Leafs or any other MLSE franchise. The only guy with a personal stake in the team is simply one voice among many.

But of the ownership group, no one is more viscerally connected to the teams than Tanenbaum. His routine rarely varies. Moments after the wail of the siren at home games, Tanenbaum bids warm farewells to the various guests and VIPs in the directors' section behind the Leafs' bench like a host at a house party. Then he makes his way out of the Platinum Club bunkers underneath the stands. Taking a right turn at the hallway, he heads for the team's dressing room, where two stainless steel doors open with an impressive *Star Trek*–like swoosh. He stops in to visit the coach's office before making his way around the room to greet the players in various stages of sweaty undress.

It's a throwback for him, and more pleasant now because he doesn't have to worry about picking up the icky gear or dodging snapped towels as he did during his time as the student manager for the Big Red at Cornell University during the early days of the Ivy League school's budding hockey dynasty, Tanenbaum's first foray into the inner sanctum of hockey. During freshman orientation week in 1964, Tanenbaum met the school's legendary hockey coach, Ned Harkness. That he was Canadian—and one of the few on campus not playing for the team—convinced Harkness to hire him as student manager of what was then the school's best and most popular team, packing them in at the 4,000-seat James Lynah Rink on cold winter nights.

It was a glamour team, but student manager was hardly a glamour position, and perhaps an odd one for a rich kid from Toronto to undertake with such enthusiasm. Tanenbaum earned his seat on the bench by picking up sweaty gear and making travel arrangement for a bunch of jocks. "It was a tough job," says Ken Dryden in an earlier interview, then the all-American goalie for Cornell, later the netminder for the dynastic Montreal Canadiens and a Leafs executive. "Guys that age aren't always the most respectful." The payoff, said Tanenbaum, was being part of the gang. "Besides," Tanenbaum said later, "winning was fun." In 1967, the team won the NCAA championship. It almost made up for missing his hometown Leafs' last Stanley Cup run. "I was studying for exams. You couldn't see the [Leafs'] games on television," he says. "I had to call home to get the scores. It was like smoke signals back in those days, but it was wonderful when they won."

While Tanenbaum has never been entirely disrespected during his run as the Leafs most ambitious minority owner, he's had his fingers rapped enough times that if he's ever able to call the shots, he'll appreciate the moment. Early on he ran afoul of Stavro as Tanenbaum was working to merge the operations of the Leafs and the Raptors, then controlled by broadcaster Allan Slaight. At one point he thought he had an agreement in principle, only to have Stavro shoot him down with a terse warning: "I make the deals around here." Their relationship became adversarial enough that Tanenbaum removed himself from the MLSE board in

May 2000, appointing uber-lawyer Dale Lastman—son of former Toronto mayor Mel Lastman and managing partner of Bay Street law firm Goodmans—to take his place. Even after the company was reorganized in 2003 and Stavro was finally bought out, Tanenbaum's influence has been less than his profile might indicate. He did manage to have the ACC's directors' lounge—the exclusive gathering place for MLSE directors and guests between the Leafs and Raptors dressing rooms—redecorated by celebrity designer Bruce Mau, with an assist from wife Judy Tanenbaum. The lounge was transformed from a dark, wood-panelled hideout for cigar smokers and single-malt drinkers to a beige-toned room reminiscent of a boutique hotel lobby or a hip new restaurant. "The new room isn't so much a reflection of Larry," said one MLSE insider. "It's just that the old one was so much a reflection of Steve." But in decisions that might have an impact on the ice, Tanenbaum has been thwarted.

He signed off on the hiring of John Ferguson, he'll acknowledge. But he was overruled on changing course when it was clear that the rookie general manager was out of his depth.

🍁

BEFORE YOU BLAME TANENBAUM for the Ferguson years, hear him out. He had a plan. Ferguson was supposed to be mentored by Quinn, who had reluctantly surrendered his general manager's title to the young upstart. Tanenbaum was the owners' public face in trying to make it work. But good luck trying to get Pat Quinn to do something he's not interested in doing. It soon became clear that Quinn was not going to lift a finger to help Ferguson, and there was nothing anyone could do about it. Not that Tanenbaum didn't try. Quinn would make his way from the ACC to Scotia Plaza, be ushered in to Tanenbaum's calming, light-filled office, and be encouraged to do as he's been asked. The selling point was the opportunity to leave a legacy to a young executive to be seen as a bridge between generations. Quinn would nod, hint he'd do better and change not a bit. "Pat always used to say yes. He was that type of guy," says one source close to the Leafs' ownership group. "He didn't argue the point. He never said John was useless or couldn't do it. He just did his own thing. That was Pat."

Tanenbaum realized it wasn't going to work six months into the experiment, but couldn't do anything to turn things around or fix the mess he'd had a hand in making. They talked around it. They wanted to give it more time. The other shareholders were wavering on it and Peddie was hardly going to push them one way or the other. Lighting a fire under Ferguson too soon would erode Peddie's own credibility. That meant it was up to Tanenbaum. "Was Larry going to go to the wall [to fire Ferguson]? The answer is no. . . . You have to decide if that's where you're going to put the line in the sand: This is it, I want this done or this partnership we have is done. [Tanenbaum] wasn't prepared to do that over that issue."

That makes two mulligans Tanenbaum would like: hiring Ferguson and not firing him. "I know that's not what he would do again," said a Tanenbaum associate. "If he saw something that's not working and it's real obvious, he'd speak up."

Maybe it was Tanenbaum, not Ferguson, who was learning on the job. In the summer of 2008, just as the economy was beginning to look like a smoking crater, Tanenbaum began the process that could one day make him the new majority owner of MLSE. With advertising revenue collapsing, Ivan Fecan, president and CEO of CTVGlobeMedia, was looking to raise cash and cut costs. The company's 15.4 percent stake in Canada's most reliable cash cow seemed like a handy source of money. Calls were made. Tanenbaum knew an opportunity when he saw one, and paid about $95 million for an additional 7.7 percent stake in the organization, thereby increasing his share to 20.5 percent, second only to Teachers' 58 percent. If and when Teachers' chooses to sell its holdings, Tanenbaum's deal with CTVGlobeMedia means that even if the remaining shareholders divided up Teachers' stake amongst themselves in proportion with their current holdings, Tanenbaum would become the largest single shareholder and gain effective control of the organization. If it happens, it will likely mark the most amicable transfer of ownership and control in nearly fifty years, since the dawn of the Ballard era. The battle for the most cherished and valuable bauble in Canadian sports has almost been won. Teachers' has never hidden its willingness to sell, and the team's status as a bulletproof cash cow means it could always be sold for the right price, particularly in a down market. At some point Tanenbaum will be in position to make his Stanley Cup vision come true. His word, and his alone, will carry the day. Leaf fans can only hope that when he speaks up, he'll have something to say.

THE LEAFS DO IT AGAIN

MARCH 1979: Days after firing coach Roger Neilson and still unable to find someone willing to work as Neilson's successor, owner Harold Ballard rehires the coach. Ballard orders him to make his return to the bench wearing a paper bag over his head, and though general manager Jim Gregory urges Neilson to go along with the gag, he declines.

DECEMBER 29, 1979: The Leafs send Lanny McDonald and Joel Quenneville to the Colorado Rockies for Pat Hickey and Wilf Paiement. Later the same day, Leafs captain Darryl Sittler instructs a club employee to unstitch the C from his jersey. McDonald, who had averaged 45 goals in the three seasons before he was dealt, goes on to score 66 goals in a season and win a Stanley Cup with the Calgary Flames. Days after the trade, players put a picture of Imlach on a dart board and commence drinking while throwing.

JANUARY 20, 1982: The Leafs trade captain Darryl Sittler to the Flyers for Rich Costello, a second-round pick (which became Peter Ihnacak) and a player to be named later, Ken Strong. Costello and Strong play a combined 27 career NHL games while Ihnacak becomes a point-a-game stalwart, albeit for the Newmarket Saints.

OCTOBER 15, 2007: In the midst of a dismal stretch of play in which Bryan McCabe is routinely booed at the Air Canada Centre, McCabe scores on his own net with 3.7 seconds remaining in overtime to give the Buffalo Sabres a 5-4 win. "He's one of the elite offensive players in the National Hockey League," says Paul Maurice, the Toronto coach of the day.

Leafs general manager, John Ferguson Jr., hears it from his predecessor and coach, Pat Quinn. The old hand was supposed to mentor the rookie GM. JFJ fired him.

Chapter Five

Blame John Ferguson Jr.
(and Peddie and Tanenbaum for hiring him)

"I honestly do not believe a Leafs GM could purchase a hockey stick without getting board approval."

— *Mark Ridout, Ajax*

WHEN 36-SIX-YEAR-OLD John Ferguson Jr. was named the general manager of the Maple Leafs on August 29, 2003, his arrival was denigrated almost as feverishly as Burke's would be celebrated just over five years later.

The *Toronto Sun* panned Ferguson's arrival before it was even made official: "The Leafs apparently have joined the other Toronto teams in turning to inexperienced leadership. Welcome to Loserville." A *Toronto Star* headline was only slightly more enthusiastic: "Looks like the same old Leafs. Don't expect much if Ferguson is GM."

But Peddie, attempting as usual to appear oblivious to the public roasting, tooted his horn for unearthing a diamond. "He is very smart, hard-working and of excellent character," Peddie told reporters. "And, as has been pointed out by many, he's also young, an asset that we value as much as Edmonton did when they hired Glen Sather at the age of 35, or the New York Islanders did when they hired Bill Torrey at the age of 38, or the Montreal Canadiens did when they hired Sam Pollock at 39."

If the media was guilty of being pre-emptively negative, perhaps it's fair to say the CEO was setting the bar a tad too high. Sather, Torrey and Pollock, after all, only won a combined eighteen Stanley Cups in their storied careers. By the time Ferguson was fired after four and a half years on the job in February 2008, he had won a grand total of six playoff games.

Blame John Ferguson Jr. for the mess the Leafs find themselves in, and you'll have a case. But while Ferguson left his post as the butt of many jokes and with a reputation as an uncommunicative stuffed shirt averse to working alongside anyone who posed a threat to his authority, it's worth remembering that the Leafs weren't the only team who saw him as viable management material. He had been a finalist for the general manager's gig of the San Jose Sharks that eventually went to Doug Wilson. After he was fired in Toronto, he was not dispatched to a leper colony or a Siberian prison. He went to work for the Sharks as the director of scouting.

Today he's on the job, on his way to Hamilton from

Toronto to scout an American Hockey League game not long after the one-year anniversary of his ouster. Ferguson weaves through traffic in his sleek Range Rover. Conversation soon turns to the influence Peddie and the board exerted over his managerial reign. Considering Ferguson was deemed tight-lipped and paranoid during his time in Toronto, as though the strengths and weaknesses of the Maple Leafs were some state secret, he turns out to be a willing conversationalist. But while Ferguson was lampooned on talk radio for his lawyerly reserve, and while Peddie has acknowledged he erred in not hiring an executive with better communication skills, Ferguson appears to be punching back. As he rolls west down Highway 401, he briefly recaps his appearance earlier that day on the sports-talk show *Off the Record*. He's got ring around the collar from the TV makeup.

"It is," he says of the broadcast business, morphing noticeably back to a man of few words when the talk turns from hockey to himself, "enjoyable."

It never looked as though Ferguson was enjoying a minute of his job as the top hockey man for one of the game's marquee teams. And that's because there were barriers in his way. Peddie, of course, has adamantly denied that he meddled in Ferguson's dealings. But there has long been a rumbling in the arena corridors that Peddie is not quite being truthful. Did the board nix, say, Ferguson's alleged plan to head off the sad ending to

Mats Sundin's Toronto career by trading the captain for some real assets? Could Ferguson have prevented Sundin's bizarre glide into a brief retirement and a midseason free-agent signing with the Vancouver Canucks that left the Leafs with nothing to show for the loss of their captain? Sundin made any speculation moot by refusing to waive his no-trade clause. Did the board refuse to okay Ferguson's other rebuilding strategies in favour of their unending insistence on short-term fixes to put a playoff qualifier on the ice? Getting warmer.

What is certain is that at the moment Peddie and the board hired Ferguson, at the moment they elevated an unknown from being a detail-oriented assistant to the big-picture chief of one of pro sport's most intensely scrutinized franchises, Ferguson was beholden to his superiors. Even though he knew, as every alert hockey man knew, that the lockout that cancelled the 2004–05 season and the new collective bargaining agreement changed the way the game was played in the league's front offices. The ground was shifting and the salary-cap era would change the way championship teams were built. He knew that. But he also knew that the men who'd just taken a leap of faith in hiring him had definitions of success that didn't begin and end with the on-ice product.

"We were trying to get a little younger, faster, trying to get more in step with what might be the new reality. But that wasn't fully embraced by the board," Ferguson says. "So it became, 'We're going to make the playoffs *and* retool.' And that challenge was significantly tougher." The problem was not that management didn't want to win. It was that they didn't want to lose.

We're in the media dining room at Hamilton's Copps Coliseum now, a meeting place for scouts and reporters that serves game-night reminders that the life of a pro-hockey lifer isn't always a five-star ride. It's a long way from the Air Canada Centre's Platinum Club, where they serve a "Platinum Burger"—$38 plus tax— that is billed on the menu as "a hand-cut Wagyu beef patty stacked with pan-seared duck *foie gras,* roasted Portobello mushrooms, truffled *pecorino* cheese, shallot jam, double-smoked bacon and ponzu *aïoli* on an Ace kaiser." Heck, it's a long way from the media room at the ACC, where there is usually a vegetable on the menu, albeit for a $12 fee. Here, the offering is free lukewarm pepperoni pizza on a Styrofoam plate.

Ferguson digs in and recalls that in board meetings in the pre-lockout days, he charted for his superiors the way the league's economic fundamentals were going to change.

"The writing was on the wall, literally, in my PowerPoint presentation," he says. "It should have been communicated more forcefully that at that time the organization was not anywhere near chock full of this young depth that you were going to need [in the post-lockout era]."

Did Ferguson make mistakes that had nothing to do with the board's vision, or lack thereof? Every talk-radio caller and Internet blogger has a list of his sins. He acknowledges that he underestimated how long the lockout would last (which made his trade for Brian Leetch something of a blunder; Ferguson had hoped the slick defenceman would be a Toronto asset in the 2004–05 season that was ultimately cancelled). Beyond the lockout, though, Ferguson said he made the board well aware of the coming economic reality: that the Leafs' chief competitive advantage—that is, big spending—was about to go the way of clutch-and-grab hockey. With the stroke of a pen, the NHL guaranteed that the lucrative trips to the playoffs would no longer be a given for deep-pocketed teams like the Leafs.

"[In reports to the board], I had question marks about the playoffs in the post-lockout era. They said, 'What does that mean?' I said, 'What it means is, if you want to keep young assets and be better in the years to come, you've got to run the risk that this club might not be able to qualify,'" says Ferguson. "And that wasn't something they were willing to embrace. And it needed to be embraced. Because you can't have mixed messages on that front. That approach needs to be embraced in the organization from top to bottom."

It never really had been embraced, of course, not when Peddie was working for the pension-plan money men who happily bathed in playoff gate receipts that amounted to more than $2 million per game. Not when Larry Tanenbaum, the chairman, was still of the mind that the playoffs were something of a lottery—as in, you can't win if you don't have a ticket. The truth is that the bottom-of-the-bracket playoff teams have had almost no chance of winning a championship. Since the NHL instituted a sixteen-team playoff tournament in 1979-80, exactly one champion has finished outside the top seven in the overall regular-season standings (in the lockout-shortened 1994-95 season, when the New Jersey Devils finished tenth and hoisted the big chalice). In other words, champions don't squeak into the playoffs and write Cinderella stories, no matter that the Leafs spent many a season squandering their future in the pursuit of such a fairy tale.

Of course, this kind of managerial dysfunction was nothing new to Leafland. Pat Quinn only handed over the keys to the general manager's office against his will after a protracted boardroom power struggle. And because Quinn wanted to retain his other job as the team's coach, it was no surprise that he supported potential GM successors with whom he shared a relationship, among them Steve Tambellini, Quinn's one-time protégé with the Vancouver Canucks, and Bob Nicholson, the longtime head of Hockey Canada with whom Quinn had teamed as coach of Canada's gold medal–winning team at the 2002 Olympics in Salt Lake City. Other candidates for the job Ferguson eventually landed included Colin Campbell, the NHL's director of hockey operations; Craig Button, the former Calgary Flames GM; Neil Smith, the former New York Rangers GM; and Ray Shero, who'd eventually end up as GM of the Pittsburgh Penguins. Even Lanny McDonald, the former Leaf, got mentioned in the discussion.

That the list took so long to pare down could perhaps be explained by the presence on the search committee of Ken Dryden. Dryden is a revered figure in hockey circles for good reason. But his record as an executive is such that, as Dryden goes about his business as a member of Parliament, all indications suggest his day is rarely, if ever, interrupted with job offers from NHL teams.

We won't offer a definitive history of his short-comings as a sports executive in this book, but here's an example of a masterwork. When Dryden hired Mike Smith to be the associate general manager in 1997 (this after Dryden interviewed Smith and others for the general manager's job and decided that the one candidate he hadn't interviewed, a man named Ken Dryden, was the ideal GM), the theory was that Dryden would learn the nitty-gritty detail of the day-to-day grind from on high, by watching his subordinates at work. And if handing out on-the-job training to a guy with one of the biggest salaries and most important portfolios in the place seemed awfully counterproductive for a so-called elite sporting organization, it wasn't even half the problem. Because Dryden was Tanenbaum's old Cornell

University chum, because Tanenbaum had an actual ownership stake in the club but enjoyed little power while Peddie had none of his own money invested but had the ear of the majority-holding Teachers', the conflict was obvious. Not surprisingly, Dryden, as Tanenbaum's surrogate, and Peddie, as the champion of the big-money interests, spent a lot of time waging a turf war for effective control of the hockey operation.

The team was having some success amid all this politicking, to be sure, surging to the Eastern Conference final against the Buffalo Sabres in 1999 and the Carolina Hurricanes in 2002. But that didn't mean everything the Leafs did made sense. Dryden hired Smith, for instance, having never met Smith face to face. And once Smith, who'd been the general manager of the Winnipeg Jets, arrived in Toronto, it didn't take him long to understand that something didn't smell quite right at the ACC. In a boardroom soap opera that played out in the headlines, Smith amounted to, in his words, "a football" kicked back and forth by Dryden and Peddie.

"I mean, I could say some things about Ken Dryden, but I really don't want to make your book a best-seller," says Smith, speaking over the line from his home in Martha's Vineyard, Massachusetts. "Ken was a loose cannon. I don't think my feelings were any different than most of the people in the hockey department back then. He tried to interfere in everything. If Ken couldn't put his name on it, he didn't want it. I don't know if anybody else will tell you that, but that's what they used to say: 'The Touch of Ken.' If he can't put his name on it, he doesn't want it.'"

Dryden, who didn't respond to an interview request for this book, barely outlasted Smith, but he was around long enough to fire him. Smith says he was terminated by Dryden, as he was interviewed by him, over the phone and while driving his wife to the hospital for cancer treatment. Asked if Dryden knew that the bad news was delivered under those circumstances, Smith says, "Well, he knew I was driving my wife to the hospital, and he knew she had cancer." Days later, Dryden was removed from the GM's post and reassigned as a senior advisor of some sort. Peddie had effectively won the battle for control (although it would take him another couple of years to oust Quinn from the GM's seat and fully reign over the hockey department long enough to bring in Ferguson). It is astonishing that so much strategizing by so many well-paid executives was deployed in a struggle that did not help the Leafs win a single game.

Says Smith, "I enjoyed working for the Leafs. My second year we went to the semifinals, and then they let me go because Ken Dryden was upset because he wasn't getting all the glory. And then they let Ken Dryden go within two days. So I really think that cost them a Stanley Cup. Because you had the goalie in Curtis Joseph. You had a good coach in Pat Quinn. You had real good leadership. I think we had the potential to win the Stanley

Cup, and then it all unravelled very quickly and they haven't made solid decisions since, really."

The decision to hire Ferguson was made in the same environment. Some critics called the ensuing summertime search a charade, as Dryden, Peddie and Quinn adopted selfless team-first postures, then worked tirelessly to advance their own interests. Some called Ferguson a compromise choice, since the club couldn't be seen to be hiring one of Quinn's favourites or one of Dryden's suggestions. But Tanenbaum, a believer in the merits of a form of psychological testing at which Ferguson was a high scorer, apparently believed in Ferguson. (And when Quinn registered his protest, says a source close to him, Tanenbaum told Quinn that if he didn't like it, he could settle on a buyout with Peddie). Peddie, for his part, had already seen the benefit of hiring an inexperienced general manager on the basketball side of the operation. During Rob Babcock's ill-fated run as GM of the Raptors, Peddie's regular two cents were a staple of the coverage of the team. Clearly, he liked talking publicly about sports, even if his credentials were dubious. And though a more seasoned executive might not stand for such attention-seeking from above—Quinn once suggested Leafs honchos "keep their traps shut" in a thinly veiled shot at Peddie—newbies are pliable.

"Everybody knows that I'm not a hockey guy, I am a business guy," Peddie told reporters at the time of the Ferguson search. "But I know the business of sports and today's sports is very big business, so [the search] was a really good exercise. I interviewed a lot of interesting people, I learned from that and I talked to a lot of the big names in hockey, so it has been a great exercise for me personally."

Ferguson, if he lacked the leverage to stand up to Peddie, didn't lack for public confidence. "Their faith in me is well placed," Ferguson said on the day he was introduced as general manager. "It will be rewarded."

Alas, though Ferguson was general manager of the team that compiled a franchise-record 103 points in the year before the NHL lockout, the team that beat the Ottawa Senators in a seven-game first-round series before falling to the Philadelphia Flyers in six games in the second round, it was all downhill from there. After that, he erred early and often. Consider the team's goaltending situation under his watch. Perhaps because Ed Belfour had been the linchpin of the Leafs' victory over the Senators in the so-called Battle of Ontario, Ferguson felt compelled to sign the 39-year-old Belfour to a new contract, even as the lockout loomed. Certainly Ferguson's belief that the work stoppage wouldn't last a full season had an impact on the decision. But no one said Ferguson was stupid, just that he was dead wrong. And Belfour hardly helped his GM's cause. He would choose to be one of the few NHL players who opted not to play, in Europe or elsewhere, during the shutdown. (Mats Sundin would be another veteran Leaf who would decide he'd rather not play hockey, given the choice.) In the end, Belfour never recaptured his form, and the Leafs ended up paying him something in the range of $8 million for less than one season of spotty work.

Because goaltending is a position ignored at an NHL team's peril—witness the inability of the talent-stacked Senators to find ultimate success while trotting out a succession of flawed netminders—Ferguson used the Leafs' first-round pick in the 2005 draft to grab another goaltender, Finnish junior sensation Tuukka Rask. He then traded Rask about a year later to the Boston Bruins for Andrew Raycroft. Yes, the Andrew Raycroft who would turn out to be the thirty-fourth-best goalie in the league in the 2006–07 season. True, he did win a record thirty-seven games for the Leafs, but only by playing just about every game. When the guy between the pipes every night has an .894 save percentage, something has to give. Raycroft was supplanted by Vesa Toskala as the Leafs' starting goalie in the following season. But to get Toskala, Ferguson traded another first-round pick, this one the thirteenth-overall selection, along with a second- and fourth-round pick. That's a lot to give up for a guy Brian Burke identified at the end of the season as a reason the Leafs didn't make the playoffs. Despite all the resources Ferguson poured into the position in just a handful of years, the Leafs find themselves essentially at ground zero in their search for a bedrock netminder. It is a dubious legacy.

For all the public outcry, there were problems behind the scenes that didn't get much attention. One was the short tenure of Craig Button, who'd been a candidate for general manager's job before Ferguson was hired and who was eventually hired by Ferguson as the team's director of player personnel. Button knew something of Ferguson's situation. In 2000, at age 37, he'd been named the general manager of the Calgary Flames, where he spent most of three seasons presiding over a decline in the club's fortunes. The Flames never made the playoffs on his watch, and he was roundly criticized for leaving the roster in a shambles. Still, Button's credentials before he became a GM were impressive. He'd been the director of scouting and was promoted to the director of player personnel for the Dallas Stars during a successful string of seasons that culminated in the Stars' 1998 Stanley Cup on a goal Sabres fans are still calling for the league to review because Brett Hull's skate was in the crease. And Button, like Ferguson, is the son of an NHL father. Jack Button was the general manager of the Pittsburgh Penguins for a time in the 1970s, and he was assistant general manager of the Washington Capitals for most of two decades until he died in 1996.

During his time in Toronto, Button, who spent 2008–09 as a commentator with the NHL Network, saw more than just a lack of managerial fortitude and fore-sight. He saw a huge company and sporting institution that thought small. And he saw Ferguson constantly bowing to the pressure to come up with short-term solutions to long-term problems.

"When John came in, it was interesting. He talked about, 'We've got to build this with draft picks and with youth.' He was hired in August of '03. And at the trade deadline of '04, first-round draft picks were flying out the door," Button says, speaking over the phone from his home in Calgary. "But that's Toronto. There's different pressures that exist. And I think they exist whether your name is Ken Dryden or Pat Quinn or Cliff Fletcher or John Ferguson. And it'll apply to Brian Burke. I believe the key part of it is you can't get caught up in the immediacy. What happens when you get caught up in the immediacy is that you don't see the forest for the trees. Therefore, a trade of a third-overall pick for Tom Kurvers occurs."

The Kurvers trade, of course, wasn't a Ferguson stroke. It happened on the watch of Floyd Smith, who dispatched what turned out to be the third-overall selection in the 1991 draft to the New Jersey Devils in a move to shore up Toronto's defence. The Devils used the pick to select Scott Niedermayer, who'd go on to anchor three Stanley Cup winners. Kurvers was traded to the Vancouver Canucks for Brian Bradley, who would go on to score 42 goals in an NHL season, albeit for the Tampa Bay Lightning, who got him for nothing when the Leafs left him unprotected in the 1992 expansion draft.

"Maple Leaf Sports and Entertainment has massive resources, which is a good thing. I've seen a real lack of foresight in the use of those resources to really gain a competitive advantage. Personnel, scouting procedures, processes, development, all those things," Button says. "I couldn't fathom how pennywise and pound-foolish they were. I mean, if development and recruiting are going to be key parts of your operation—and they need to be—well, I'll tell you what, you blanket the earth. You use your resources. If you can't spend some of your resources on player acquisition (because of the salary cap), you spend it on developing players. You make sure you're as sharp as anything. In my time there, I thought that was severely lacking."

Ferguson, sitting high above the ice at Hamilton's minor-league rink, making meticulous notes on the action below, glances up at the press-box video monitor. It's showing a Leafs game, and Ferguson begins a rumination on the current state of his former employer. "Clearly the organization now, whether it's through capitulation, whatever else, is clearly on board. The manager has a six-year deal. The coach has a four-year deal," he says with the touch of admiring envy you might expect from a man who never enjoyed that kind of long-term job security. Ferguson can't resist a playful jab at Burke's build-it-from-the-basement philosophy. "When you're not trying to win," he says, "it's hard to underachieve."

Even when the Ferguson regime was on the verge of getting it right, they sometimes got it wrong. Consider the case of Fabian Brunnstrom, the Swedish forward with whom the Leafs shared a strange off-ice dance. Brunnstrom signed with the Dallas Stars in 2007, and he played regularly with the big club with modest results that saw him spend some time in the minors during the 2008–09 campaign. But the Swede's eventual fate as a pro isn't particularly vital to this anecdote. What's important to understand is that, in the fall of 2007, Brunnstrom's name was a veritable buzzword everywhere from hockey message boards to NHL executive offices. What made him so attractive? He was a classic late bloomer who hadn't been drafted by an NHL club, which made him an unrestricted free agent. And so, at age twenty-two, he was suddenly among the most-talked-about players in Sweden's elite league.

NHL scouts had seen this kind of phenomenon before and largely ignored it, which allowed the Ottawa Senators to draft an unheralded Swede named Daniel Alfredsson with the 133rd-overall pick in the 1994 draft, a move that turned out to lay a key piece of the foundation for a Senators team that became, for a while, a perennial contender with Alfredsson as captain.

The frustrating thing for various members of the Ferguson scouting staff in Toronto was that, while most of the league was fawning over Brunnstrom by November of 2007, the Leafs had tracked him down long before. Toronto, for all of the criticisms that have been levelled at its scouting department over the years, had made a key investment in bird-dogging in the 1990s, when they signed Swedish scout Thommie Bergman to be their director of European scouting. Bergman was a pioneering player in the 1970s as the first Swedish defenceman to play in the NHL, a title often erroneously given to Borje Salming of the Maple Leafs. And Bergman, in his post-playing career, had carved out a reputation as a man with a keen eye for talent. The Leafs, looking to shore up their global scouting arm, had gone to considerable trouble to secure Bergman's services, paying a tampering fine to the NHL for stealing him away from Anaheim. It was considered a move of rare genius by some insiders, but it got little in the way of notice.

When Bergman saw Brunnstrom playing for Boras of Hockey Allsvenskan, Sweden's second-best league, he knew the kid was bound for bigger things. Convinced of Brunnstrom's talent, the scout finally summoned Button to Europe to see for himself. And as they continued to watch the prospect—at one point buying tickets to a game (rather than alerting other scouts to their presence by requesting a pass) and sitting among the fans wearing big coats and hats so as not to be recognized—Button soon agreed with Bergman that Brunnstrom had NHL potential. The developmental plan, which seemed to make sense to Brunnstrom's camp and to Bergman, would be to sign the player to a contract and have him play the 2007–08 season in the Swedish Elite League. He would play for Farjestad, a respected club where he would be coached by Hakan Loob, a Swede who'd earned a Stanley Cup ring with the Calgary Flames in 1989 and a man who knows what it takes to make the jump to the NHL.

"It was a no-brainer," says Button, looking back. "I mean, here was a free agent you can sign for next to nothing? It's a no-brainer."

But when Bergman brought the plan to Ferguson and the GM's lieutenant, Mike Penny, the no-brainer became a flat-out no.

"Mike Penny, with John Ferguson right there, said, 'There's no fucking way we're fucking signing a guy and having him play in fucking Sweden. What the fuck is this bullshit?'" says Button. "I'm sitting there thinking, 'Okay. Don't listen to me. That's okay. But you hired this guy, Thommie Bergman, and this is his job, to find talent in Europe, and this is how he gets treated?' But that's exactly what was said.

"Here you have a guy [Bergman] doing exactly what you want. He's doing it right, getting all the information. I'm just corroborating what he said. It was such a no-brainer to sign [Brunnstrom] for the cost. And they completely missed the opportunity. . . . They'd never seen him play and [the idea] was completely dismissed. Not partly dismissed. Not 'Let's see him play.' Completely dismissed."

That's not the way Ferguson remembers the conversation. But he doesn't deny that, months later, when Brunnstrom was still unsigned and playing for Farejstad, the Leafs were among the teams suddenly expressing interest in his services. By that point, though, Brunnstrom's camp was said to be aware of the initial rebuff by the Leafs' higher-ups. And sure enough, just as Brunnstrom gave Toronto a pass, Button wasn't long for the Leafs. Button called the Brunnstrom affair "one of the straws that breaks the camel's back." But there were others. He didn't agree with the club's decision to move the American Hockey League club from St. John's, Newfoundland, to Toronto's Ricoh Coliseum.

"I think it's the dumbest thing they ever could have done. Putting [prospects] under the scrutiny of Toronto? I can't think of anything dumber. How do you live in a city like Toronto when you're a young player making $50,000 a year? But that was a business-side decision. They thought they were going to make a ton of money off the Marlies. They thought they'd make something like $3 million or $4 million a year. And they're losing $3 million or $4 million a year. So they were off by $6- or $8 million."

Above all, perhaps, Button didn't feel he was making a contribution. Perhaps because Ferguson was afraid of involving anyone who could be seen as a threat to his power in the decision-making process— and Button, a former NHL GM, could certainly have qualified as a threat—Button says his suggestions fell on unreceptive ears.

"A big reason I left is there's got to be a fit. When you don't feel you're contributing, when you don't feel anybody's paying attention even, it's difficult to stick around," says Button. "I cannot begin to tell you how non-communicative John Ferguson and Mike Penny were. I'm talking, not even, 'Good idea.' You'd send stuff to them—nothing. Somebody asked me once, 'What's John like in private?' I said, 'Exactly like he is in public.' And I'm not trying to rip on John. I think he was over-whelmed. I think he was like a deer in the headlights and he didn't know what to do. But again, was that John's fault? Or was that Richard Peddie's fault? To me, Richard Peddie deserves all the blame for putting that person in that spot."

Ferguson, for his part, doesn't blame anyone. Soon he will be driving back to Toronto after watching the Manitoba Moose beat the Hamilton Bulldogs. For now, he is in the Copps Coliseum press box defending the abilities of the players he signed with an admirable (and some would say delusional) loyalty. In 2008–09, Nik Antropov would become the target of harsh words from Burke and coach Ron Wilson. But just weeks before Burke and Wilson lash out at Antropov, Ferguson defends his faith in the big Kazakh.

"Antropov's deal is expiring, and at the time I signed him he was an unrestricted free agent and there were people saying, 'We have to let him go.' I said, 'We put ten years of development into this guy. He's finally start-ing to pay off. We can't let him go,'" Ferguson says. "And as it turns out, we probably should have signed him for longer. The $2 million is great, but it was only two years. For some people, too long. But ultimately, too short." Not too short for the New York Rangers, though, who picked up Antropov at the trade deadline for a second-round pick. Leaf fans watched in horror as the towering forward immediately started putting up big numbers during the Rangers' successful push for the playoffs.

Ferguson goes on to talk about Tomas Kaberle, who would be the Leafs' lone representative at the All-Star Game in Montreal in 2009, with the same affection. "The Kaberle deal has huge value. Tomas Kaberle, at his age, at his time on the ice, at his capabilities, at $4.25 million, you do not find it in this league. It just doesn't happen. [Brian] Campbell [the Blackhawks defenceman who Ferguson would suggest is a comparable talent] last year signed for just over $7 million."

And what of Bryan McCabe, whose Toronto tenure concluded amidst a chorus of boos at the ACC as the defenceman made embarrassing gaffe after embarrass-ing gaffe?

Suddenly Ferguson is less talkative. "McCabe at $5.75 million? More than what you want to spend at the time, no question about it." But McCabe is thriving in

Florida, as he convalesces from his crippling case of Blue and White Disease.

"I'm a realist," says Ferguson, at the wheel of his Range Rover again and looking down the road with an eye in the rear-view. "I'm very confident in what I know, the professionalism with which I handle myself.... It was always in our hands. I take full responsibility for everything we did as the manager, because the manager has to, and I make no excuse for what transpired. I believe it was my job then to make a more, let's say, fervent, consistent pitch to get the board to say, 'This is what we should have done.' Hey, those are things you learn. Those are things you learn and that's something I've learned and I've taken from the five, or just under five years, as a manager. I take pride in my work, my record, my career. I was assistant general manager at 29. I was general manager at 36. If I'd have been an NHL player and played longer, it would have happened later, but when I went back to law school that was my goal. I wanted to be a manager within five years of graduating from law school. Ambitious? Yes. Not entirely out of the question. I think it became somewhere about seven years or eight years.

"I've always been able to state clearly with conviction that I don't believe there's anyone who works harder, has more experience in the different aspects of the game, whether it's as an agent, a scout, a player, an assessor of talent, managing a draft or an amateur scouting or pro scouting group, or negotiating deals. That breadth of experience has put me in a place that made me a candidate for other jobs before I took the Toronto job, and will keep me a candidate for jobs in the future. But the job I've got right now is the sole focus of my energy, and it's a tremendous organization with a tremendous management team. Dougie Wilson I've known for years in this business, and we have a great deal of respect for his talents. Maybe it's going to put me in a position to be considered elsewhere down the road."

In Ferguson's quest for another shot at front-office stardom, "maybe" is the operative word. A second chance is hardly guaranteed. But surely Leafs fans, though they overwhelmingly applauded Ferguson's ouster, can't begrudge a man for holding out hope that a better job, a career-defining find, a championship roster, could be waiting around the coming curve.

THE LEAFS DO IT AGAIN

APRIL 4, 1982: The Leafs, 7–1 losers to the Flyers, end a season in which they win 20 of 80 games on a five-game losing streak. They miss the playoffs for the first time in nine springs.

APRIL 7, 1985: The Leafs cap their worst season since Conn Smythe bought the team in 1927, registering a league-worst 20 victories and 48 points.

Bill Derlago wins the Molson Cup for most three-star selections during the campaign.

APRIL 2001: In the lead-up to the Leafs–Senators play-off series, Ottawa mayor Bob Chiarelli accuses CBC broadcasters of pro-Toronto bias. Colour commentator Harry Neale responds in an interview that if his commentary isn't good enough for Ottawans, "they can take a big bite out of my ass."

Bobby Orr, maybe the greatest player of all time, grew up in the Leafs' backyard at a time when access to young talent was a real advantage for NHL clubs. In accordance with the finest of Leafs traditions, Orr played his entire NHL career somewhere else.

Chapter Six
Find Hope in a Young Star

"I have been a Leaf fan for a long, long, long, long time and it makes me sick to see all the other teams have a young star and never on the Leafs."

—Jeff Barry, West Guilford

SURE, IT WOULD BE GREAT to have a visionary GM or a committed owner. But let's not forget that games are decided and legacies determined not by middle-aged men with their ties loosened and their shirtsleeves rolled up as they negotiate trades and contracts, but by the guys who actually play the fastest, toughest game on the planet. So, fine, the Leafs haven't had the brains to make it back to a Stanley Cup final. But neither have they had the hands. They haven't had the one commodity in sports that sometimes overcomes everything else: those transcendent, once-or-twice-in-a-generation talents that capture imaginations and galvanize championship teams.

Measure it any way you like. Measure it with awards. Since Dave Keon won the Conn Smythe Trophy for his MVP performance in the 1967 playoffs, few Leafs have counted themselves as winners of a short list of major NHL trophies. A Leaf hasn't won the Hart Memorial Trophy as the league's MVP since Ted Kennedy claimed the prize in 1955. (And let's be honest; Kennedy didn't make the first or second NHL all-star teams that year, which is not exactly something to be ashamed of, given that roster spots were handed to the likes of Maurice Richard, Jean Beliveau, Doug Harvey and Terry Sawchuk, but it is hard not to conclude that Kennedy won the award in an era when they occasionally gave the Hart to someone who led his team, if not in scoring, then in spirit.) A Leaf hasn't won the Vezina Trophy for excellence in goaltending since Johnny Bower and Sawchuk split the award in 1965, back when the award was still given to the netminders who allowed the fewest goals in a season. (The Vezina criteria changed in 1981–82, and the award is now given to the best goalie in the league as selected by NHL general managers. The Jennings Trophy goes to the goalie or goalies with the fewest goals against.) A Leaf hasn't won a Calder Trophy as the league's top rookie since Brit Selby did in 1966. Selby, who had 27 points that year, would never have a better season for Toronto than his glorious first campaign.

There have been exceptions. Alexander Mogilny did win one a trophy as a Leaf—but he didn't win it for, say, leading the league in goal scoring, as he did by scoring 76 goals in 77 games as a member of the Buffalo Sabres in 1992–93. He won the Lady Byng Memorial Trophy for being deemed the league's most gentlemanly player in 2002–03. And Doug Gilmour won the Selke Trophy as the league's top defensive forward in 1992–93.

Measure it with scoring totals. When Gilmour's number was honoured by the Leafs in February 2009, he stood 17th on the NHL's all-time scoring list, the highest among former Leafs. But Gilmour scored only 452 of his career 1,414 regular-season points in Toronto, or 32 percent. Dave Andreychuk's 1,338 career points will probably keep him among the top 30 all-time scorers for years to come, but he scored a mere 16 percent of his points for the Leafs. As for players who spent the bulk of their careers in Toronto, Mats Sundin, who passed Andreychuk to stand 25th on the list at the end of the 2008–09 season, tops the charts. And while Sundin was certainly a bona fide first-line centre and a class act, he was never confused with the best players of his era. He topped out as a member of the NHL's second all-star team. He never finished higher than fourth in the league's scoring standings. He led the league in a significant statistical category exactly once, in 2003–04, when his 10 game-winning goals were the NHL's most. And he never enjoyed a 100-point season in Toronto. Then again, only two Leafs in history, Sittler and Gilmour, have managed that feat. A single edition of a single team, the 1985–86 Edmonton Oilers, boasted four players with point totals in the triple digits. Those Oilers, of course, won the Stanley Cup.

Measure it any way you like. When *The Hockey News* published its ranking of the 100 greatest players in NHL history in 1998, compiling a list based on the opinions of select writers and broadcasters, Sawchuk, the peerless goaltender who led the Leafs to their 1967 triumph, ranked 9th and Jacques Plante, the goalie-mask innovator who played some twilight seasons with the Leafs in the 1970s, was 13th. Heroes of the Leafs' 1960s teams cracked the top 90, among them Red Kelly (22nd) and Frank Mahovlich (26th), Tim Horton (43rd), Dave Keon (69th) and Johnny Bower (87th). But as for players who wore the Maple Leaf in their prime in the post-1967 era, Borje Salming led the way at 74th. Darryl Sittler came 93rd. It was difficult to make a case for anyone else.

Who is the greatest Leaf of the post-1967 era? It's probably a toss-up between Eric Lindros, Ed Belfour and Brian Leetch. Lindros was the game's best player for a time in the 1990s (although when he got to Toronto in 2005, he was well past his best-before date). Belfour was the league's best goalie in stretches of the 1990s, and he won a Stanley Cup with the Dallas Stars in 1999. And while he was in his career's final throes when he came to Toronto, Belfour almost single-handedly beat the Ottawa Senators in a memorable playoff series in 2004. What other post-1967 Leaf can claim that as an achievement?

Leetch, a two-time Norris Trophy winner and a Stanley Cup champion with the New York Rangers, played fifteen games for the Leafs at age 35.

Given that not-so-illustrious habit of employing sub-stars, it's understandable why one of the most talked-about hockey players in Leafland for most of the past few years has not played a game for the team. John Tavares, a teenager from Oakville who spent the bulk of his major junior career playing in nearby Oshawa before he was traded to the London Knights in the lead-up to the Ontario Hockey League's 2009 postseason, grew up a Leaf fan before he became a Leaf fan's fantasy. He had also been the consensus number-one pick in the 2009 draft in the minds of many NHL scouts from the day he began his career in the OHL, a wildly talented 14-year-old boy among men, nearly five years before he'd be eligible to be drafted into the world's best league.

Every time the Leafs won a game in 2008–09, when coach Ron Wilson pushed his troops through hard practices with high expectations, the sanest of Leafs fans were justified in wondering if a victory in the next game would mean anything other than a slimmer chance at landing Tavares. (In hockey's socialist draft-pick dispersal system, the club with the worst regular-season record has the best odds, a one-in-four chance, of winning the first-overall pick in the draft lottery. Only the bottom five clubs in the league standings have any chance at all of winning the first-overall pick. The other nine non-playoff teams can move up a maximum of four places in the draft from their finishing order. So the Leafs, who spent much of the season hovering in about sixth- or seventh-last place, were playing just a little too well for their own good.) Every time Burke insisted that tanking was not an option, anyone who dreamed of rebuilding around Tavares was justified in wondering why not.

The Leafs weren't the only ones who wanted Tavares, of course. When Tavares starred for Canada at the 2009 World Junior Championship in Ottawa, fans brought signs to the game that spoke of a collective wish for Tavares to join the then-struggling Senators (although the Sens, it was obvious to most watchers, really needed most of their help on defence and in goal).

Still, the prospect of watching Tavares for the coming handful of seasons was far more tantalizing than the idea of drafting, say, Victor Hedman, the six-foot-five Swedish defenceman who was, in the notebooks of many scouts, the best rearguard available in the 2009 draft and, by virtue of the dearth of talent at one of the game's key positions, a more bankable commodity than Tavares. And that's because Tavares could wow a crowd in a way that few defencemen ever will, making plays even he can't explain.

Witness the scene a few days before Christmas 2008, at Hamilton's Copps Coliseum. Tavares was playing in a world junior tune-up game against Slovakia. Canada would go on to win in a walk, 7–0, but even if nobody remembers the score, fans will have a hard time forgetting The Goal, which will live as a YouTube classic for years to come. With the puck fluttering in the air alongside the net but already past the Slovakian goal line, Tavares batted it out of the air exactly twice: once to bring the puck back to the scorer's side of the goal line, essentially passing it to himself for a second mid-air whack, this one tucking the puck between the goaltender and the right-hand post.

"Just had some good hand-eye coordination," Tavares told reporters after he was named Canada's player of the game. "Some of that comes from playing lacrosse and working after practice, fooling round. Sometimes those things come into play and help you out. It was a nice one to score. The guys will be bugging me about that one for a few days. . . . I still haven't seen it so it will be nice to see it. Definitely wowed myself."

That display of physical genius was hardly a fluke. Tavares's gift with a stick and a puck or a ball and a lacrosse stick is the stuff of local legend that will soon enough go global. Michael Del Zotto, who has known Tavares for most of their adolescence, played with Tavares in Oshawa and accompanied him in the deal that sent both players to London, sketched out a typical scene after practice.

"You wouldn't believe some of the stuff he can do," Del Zotto says. "I remember one practice, he went on a one-on-one with one of our younger guys. He skated up to him, flicked it over the defenceman's head and scored. I mean, he's skating at full speed, flips it over the guy's head, retrieves it on the other side and scores. He does that and guys on our team don't even say anything. Their eyes just shoot right open and 'Wow.' That's all you can say. I don't know how he comes up with this stuff."

So the kid's hands weren't a question mark. When he broke Wayne Gretzky's record for points by a 16-year-old, it was whispered that the league might make an exception on its draft-eligibility rules to get Tavares into the NHL a year early. There was no precedent for this in the league, but Hockey Canada and the Canadian Hockey League had allowed Tavares to be drafted as an under-age 14-year-old by inventing a so-called "exceptional player" rule. He'd spent most of his young life, in fact, as a boundary pusher. When he was 13 he played Junior A hockey against players as old as 21. When he was 15 he spent an OHL season compiling 45 goals and 77 points, which was precisely five more points than another 15-year-old member of the Oshawa Generals had scored some four decades earlier—a spindly defenceman by the name of Bobby Orr. Brad Selwood, the former Leaf who coached Tavares in Oshawa for the bulk of his junior career, once estimated that Tavares possessed the "tenacity of Davey Keon" and the "anticipation of a Gordie Howe."

If you knew anything about Toronto's long-time failure to hook an era's biggest fish, you would have had your doubts that the Leafs would ever land Tavares. Toronto missed the boat on Bobby Orr—only the game's greatest player of all time in the estimation of many esteemed observers—despite the fact that Orr, like his father and his grandfather and most Ontario kids in the post-war era, grew up worshipping the club. They missed the boat on Orr even though former Leaf Bucko McDonald coached the kid, even though Anthony Gilchrist, one of Orr's other minor-hockey coaches, was an old army friend of Punch Imlach, the Toronto coach of the moment. Gilchrist wrote Imlach a letter in which he touted the 12-year-old Orr as a burgeoning combination of Doug Harvey, the Canadiens all-star defenceman, and Gordie Howe, the Red Wings juggernaut. He implored Imlach to send a scout to watch the kid. He even included a rundown of Orr's coming schedule, noting that the young man would be playing in Barrie, a short drive from Maple Leaf Gardens, in the days ahead.

"It might pay to have one of your men look him over in Barrie and place him on your list before Hap Emms sees him," Gilchrist wrote to Imlach, "or I feel sure it will be too late."

The Leafs didn't exactly jump to the pump, even though Imlach had seen Orr with his own eyes when the kid played at a peewee tournament at Maple Leaf Gardens not long before the letter arrived. Orr has said the Leafs weren't the only club who glimpsed him as a pre-teen and considered him too small. While the Boston Bruins would soon be moving relative mountains to land Orr—sponsoring the entire Parry Sound minor hockey system in order to get the 12-year-old on their so-called "sponsor list," paying him an unprecedented signing bonus of $10,000, then allowing Orr to commute from Parry Sound to Oshawa for his rookie season with the Generals—the Leafs sent back what amounted to a form letter from the desk of Bob Davidson, Toronto's chief scout. Davidson promised to keep the kid's name on file.

"(W)hen he gets to be fourteen or fifteen we will contact him and, if he is good enough, I would recommend a hockey scholarship for him here in Toronto," Davidson wrote. "I appreciate your interest in the Maple Leaf Hockey Club and hope we can win that Stanley Cup. I hope that some day Bob Orr will be playing for the Maple Leafs."

He never played for the Leafs, of course, and perhaps that's as much to do with the entrepreneurial drive of a single Bruins scout as it is to do with the Leafs' slothful arrogance. Wren Blair, the bird dog who was among the first big-league scouts on the scene in Parry Sound, formed a relationship with Orr's parents, Doug and Arva, that would eventually lead to young Bobby pledging his allegiance to the black and gold. (It's interesting to note that Blair, in a long-term recruitment project that saw him repeatedly visit Parry Sound, would come to the Orr household bearing gifts, among them tickets to Leafs games.)

"Wren Blair—he's a good talker," Orr would say on the November night in 2008 when his number 2 jersey was finally retired in Oshawa. "And Wren spent many days in Parry Sound trying to convince my parents to send me here."

All Orr would do, of course, is reimagine the game, become the first (and still the only) defenceman to win the Art Ross Trophy as the league's leading scorer, win the Norris Trophy eight straight times and lead the Bruins, an NHL minnow before Orr arrived, to two Stanley Cups.

"Like all kids growing up in Ontario, I watched the Leafs play each Saturday on *Hockey Night in Canada* and listened to Foster Hewitt on the radio," Orr would tell Howard Berger years later. "They were my favourite team because I saw them every week. I hardly knew anything about the Bruins. So I'm sure my parents wouldn't have been too disappointed if Toronto had shown the same amount of interest in me that Boston did."

How did the Leafs miss?

"My people," Stafford Smythe would later fume, "were too goddamn stupid."

The Leafs had a chance to get Wayne Gretzky, too. And yes, it's true that in the summer of 1996, when Gretzky expressed a keen interest in joining the Leafs, the Great One was 35 years old and long past his prime and no longer the most prolific scorer in the game. Still, when it all went sour—when it became clear that the Leafs had better things to do with their money, like build a war chest for a new arena—Gretzky landed with the New York Rangers, where the old codger managed to put together a 97-point campaign, four more points than the Leafs' leading scorer, Mats Sundin, put on the ledger.

The beauty of the Gretzky deal—and Number 99 later told Damien Cox of the *Toronto Star* that there were a few weeks when it looked the deal would "definitely" happen—was that it wasn't the way the Leafs usually did business. Sure, they would be bringing in a grizzled veteran well past his prime. They did that all the time. The difference was that they wouldn't be shipping away a slew of young talent and draft picks to a lucky competitor to do it. This was a deal that would cost the Leafs the one thing they've almost always had in surplus: money.

And for once they'd be trading on their grand tradition in the name of more than profit. Gretzky, after all, was looking at offers from around the NHL, some of which far outweighed anything the Leafs had on the table. But Gretzky had a sentimental attachment to the Leafs and their famous arena, which he has called "my Augusta National, my Yankee Stadium, the one place on earth where hockey—my game—most deserved to be played."

It was at the Gardens that Gretzky, who grew up in Brantford, Ontario, saw his first NHL game at age six. (He went with his grandmother, who would soon rise to fame as one of Gretzky's first goaltenders; the pair sat in the last row of the greys to watch the Leafs and the California Golden Seals). When the kid who would come to be called The Great One left Brantford at 14 to play for the Toronto Young Nationals, he billeted with a family whose son had once played for the Toronto Marlboros, the minor-hockey affiliate of the NHL club. In those days members of the "Marlies" organization could get into Leafs games for a dollar, simply by wearing their team jacket at the ticket window. So young Wayne would borrow the family jacket, take the subway to the Gardens, pay his dollar and sidle up to the boards to watch the warm-ups.

"It was wonderful," Gretzky recounted in the introduction to Thomas Smythe's *Centre Ice*. "For a buck I got to stand there and watch the greatest players in the world do the most amazing things with pucks. That's when I first started dreaming seriously about one day being in this same league, playing in this very same building."

He played in the Gardens many times, of course, but never for the home side.

"And you know, the ridiculous part is Vancouver was offering me $8 million a season," Gretzky told Cox in 2004. "But I wanted to be a Leaf in the worst way. I told Cliff, 'I'll do whatever it takes to make it work. You can defer my salary for twenty-five years if you have to. Whatever it takes to get the deal done.' But he couldn't get the deal done."

He couldn't get the deal done because money, at that point in the club's history, was in short supply. Stavro was having financial problems of his own, among them a court decision that forced the grocer to pay out millions of dollars to the charities that had been named in Harold Ballard's will.

The dream, for the Leafs, never seems to come true. Even when they've had a diamond, they've found a way to lose him into the rough. Take Bernie Parent, the goaltender who was acquired in a rare master-stroke trade. Parent was property of the Philadelphia Flyers in 1971, but the Flyers already had their share of goal-tending talent. They made a deal with the Leafs for front-line help in the personage of Mike Walton, among others. Parent teamed with his boyhood hero, Jacques Plante, the pioneering netminder who was finishing out his career with the Leafs and whose mentorship proved useful to the young Parent. But while Parent played well for the Leafs, he was among a number of NHLers who would be faced with a choice. The rival World Hockey Association was opening its doors for what would be a memorable run. Parent was an early target of their recruitment, but like a lot of players, he wasn't necessarily inclined to jump to the uncertainty of a fledgling league.

"I was making $25,000 a year at the time. I had an offer of $110,000 from the WHA [World Hockey Association] but I would have signed again with the Leafs for $40,000," Parent told the *Toronto Star* years later. "That wasn't very much but the owner wouldn't give it to me."

Parent's time in the WHA didn't last long. The club he signed with, the Miami Screaming Eagles, never played a game. It wasn't long before the franchise moved to become the Philadelphia Blazers, who played before sparse crowds in a pit of an arena. Before the 1972–73 WHA playoffs were over he was mired in another contract dispute and looking to return to the NHL. But he did not wish to return to the Leafs. So Toronto traded him back to the Flyers for Doug Favell. Favell would have needed to have a pretty stellar career to make that trade look good for the Leafs in hindsight. Parent was the irreplaceable piece on the gap-toothed Broad Street Bullies teams that won two Stanley Cups. How important was Parent to those Philadelphia squads? His back-to-back performances as winner of the Vezina Trophy as the league's top goaltender and the Conn Smythe Trophy as the playoff MVP pretty much tell the tale. And Doug Favell? He ended up playing three seasons with the Leafs, though he appeared in only three games in 1975–76, his final campaign in blue and white, and posted a 5.63 goals-against average.

There is always hope, of course, in youth. And the Leafs finally landed a top-five draft pick worth dreaming about in 2008. Luke Schenn spent the 2008–09 season representing the future, the only so-called untouchable on a squad of wholly moveable Leafs, a rugged defenceman whose skill set and poise pointed to long-term success in the world's best league. Never mind that there were those who didn't understand why the Leafs, in a so-called rebuilding year, were putting him through the big-league paces (and burning up a year of his entry-level contract) at the tender age of 18. Who could know what a season in Toronto could do to a kid from Saskatoon who was being cast as a solution to an age-old problem? Who could guess what the grind of an NHL campaign could do to a teenaged physique, no matter that Schenn's was more chiselled than most? And who was surprised when Schenn went down with a knee injury that kept him out of the lineup for a few weeks in the season's dog days? Still, Schenn represented a rare commodity in Leafs Nation: a draft pick with a future, a candidate to one day maybe, possibly, hopefully win the Norris Trophy as the league's best defenceman. Sure, that's an intoxicating dream, because no player has ever won the Norris in a Leafs uniform. So it's probably not surprising that Toronto fans wanted to see the kid play right away.

THE LEAFS DO IT AGAIN

JUNE 1986: Leafs use the sixth-overall pick in the entry draft to select Vincent Damphousse, who'll go on to a fine eighteen-year career in which he plays in three All-Star Games. None of the Leafs' next nineteen first-round selections will repeat his success.

DECEMBER 1986: After reportedly paying more than $200,000 in bribes to secure Miroslav Ihnacak's defection from Czechoslovakia, Ihnacak, the younger brother of Leafs regular Peter, scores a goal in his Toronto debut. He goes on to score just seven more in an NHL career that lasts all of 56 games.

FEBRUARY 22, 1988: Leafs lose 4–2 in Minnesota. "There's a bunch of snot noses here trying to get people fired," says John Brophy.

Jim Leech, CEO of the Ontario Teachers' Pension Plan, majority owner of the Leafs.
There. Now you can't call the ownership group faceless.

Chapter Seven

Blame Teachers'

"The Ontario Teachers' Pension Fund is, and always has been, an anchor tied to the Toronto Maple Leafs' neck. Too bad there's no way to cut the rope. What an awful, frustrating time to be a Leafs fan."

— *Jon Harding, Calgary*

THE PULSING HEART of Leafs Nation lies, unquestionably, at the foot of Bay Street in the Air Canada Centre, where every home game since the building opened for hockey on February 20, 1999, has been sold out. The soul, unfortunately, left the body long ago.

While the Leaf faithful are dreaming dreams of Johnny Bower flopping around in the crease and helmet-less players in wool sweaters patrolling the ice, of Bobby Baun winning a Stanley Cup on a broken leg and other traditions the franchise has been built upon, if you listen closely you can hear a steady gurgling noise—the sound the river of profits generated by the club's passionate and massive fan base makes as it flows straight north from the ACC and comes to rest at a simple office on the northern periphery of the city: the home of the Ontario Teachers' Pension Plan.

The holding pond for that river of cash is 5650 Yonge Street, far from the bustle of the nation's financial markets. But the distance is as telling as it is economical. The mirror-fronted North American Centre at the northwest corner of Yonge and Finch costs about $40 per square foot. A comparable property on Bay Street leases for about $60. Considering the OTPP leases 231,000 square feet of office space in the North American Centre, it's a potential savings of $4.6-million annually. Those savings are invested at the OTPP's typical rate of return and fund the retirement needs of more than a few of the 280,000 teachers the plan services. Sure they could probably justify a flashier address, but that's not the way they think at the OTPP. Which must be very reassuring if you teach in the public school system in Ontario and are contemplating retirement. And if you're thinking about Stanley Cups? Well, maybe not.

They don't throw money around at Teachers', that's for sure. While Larry Tanenbaum has a driver who shuttles him from his sumptuous home in Forest Hill to his office at King and Bay, and a private jet for journeys abroad, OTPP chief executive officer Jim Leech takes the subway to meetings with Bay Street power brokers, and Teachers' executives fly economy class for flights under two hours. No, life at Teachers' is not sexy by Bay Street standards. Using the bonus money to buy a new Porsche, basic transportation for Richard Peddie, would be considered a faux pas. Instead, there is a tight focus on meeting their fiduciary duty. And while the Teachers' web site is remarkably clear and easy to navigate—the better for its members to have access to sound information about their retirement—references to winning Stanley Cups appear nowhere.

Teachers' loyalties were made plain in May 1994, when the NHL's board of governors reviewed the pension fund's purchase of a 49 percent stake in what was then Maple Leaf Gardens Ventures, the Steve Stavro–controlled holding company that owned the Leafs and Gardens. Claude Lamoureux, Teachers' chief executive officer and primary architect of its innovative investment strategy, recalls that there were two items on the agenda when he and Stavro arrived at the league offices in New York. The first was to excommunicate from the lodge disgraced Los Angeles Kings owner Bruce McNall. It was a relative formality, if not a welcome order of business. But the popular former chairman of the league's board of governors was on the run from creditors and on borrowed time before eventually winding up in jail for fraud to the tune of an estimated $236 million. So Lamoureux had to cool his heels for a moment before eventually getting the thumbs-up. "It took as long for them to accept us as it took for them to throw [McNall] out," says Lamoureux. "I said, 'Gosh, he's a thief. I don't think we're thieves here.'"

Quite the opposite. In the rough-and-tumble alleys of big business, Teachers' is the proverbial Boy Scout. As part of the fallout from the "tech wreck"—the 2001 stock market implosion that vapourized billions in wealth and eventually exposed companies like Nortel as little more than the fantasies of creative accountants— Teachers' began to use its clout to clean up the corporate governance practices of Canadian public companies. Lamoureux helped found the Canadian Coalition for Good Governance, the self-proclaimed "voice of the shareholder," in 2003. Even in 1994 there was no reason that Teachers' would fail an integrity test, certainly not one administered by the NHL.

The problem was that no one, not even NHL commissioner Gary Bettman, knew exactly what to make of a pension fund acting on behalf of a teachers' union buying an NHL team. Flamboyant entrepreneurs making a splash with other people's occasionally ill-gotten money? That's an NHL tradition! The glorious Edmonton Oilers dynasties of the mid-1980s might have been the highest expression of hockey aesthetics seen before or since, but off the ice they were an odious financial swamp run by Peter Pocklington, who left the team's business affairs in a smoking heap. McNall's case was only the most ambitious of that particular approach, as he used a web of lies to amass millions, some of which he used to buy racehorses, others he used to buy Wayne Gretzky (for $18 million from Pocklington, who won four Stanley Cup rings thanks to The Great One, but eventually needed the cash). Gretzky carried the Kings to the 1993 Stanley Cup final (breaking the hearts of Leafs fans in the process) before McNall's financial house of cards came tumbling down. And as the more recent legal troubles besetting Nashville Predators minority owner William "Boots" Del Biaggio—who allegedly qualified for the loan he used to buy his share of the Predators by forging documents—rogue owners with questionable motives and means are simply an unfortunate aspect of the NHL fabric, the boardroom equivalent of face washes after the whistle and checking from behind.

Bettman has met his share of scoundrels. Not a problem. But that doesn't mean the NHL's not-so-diligent due diligence process is a rubber stamp. "One of the questions Bettman asked was, 'You work for a union—and obviously there's a union in the NHL—so how is that going to affect how you vote?'" recalls Lamoureux, who quickly set the commissioner straight. "I said I don't work for a union. I work for the members of a pension plan. It's a big distinction. My role is to do what's best for the members of the plan and the tax-payers of the province. That's it." They got the board's approval, and a new era in Maple Leafs hockey began.

When Lamoureux got on the plane to New York, he was ostensibly Steve Stavro's quiet money. But it was the kind of quiet money that wielded a massive financial clout. With a total value of $34 billion in 1994, when Teachers' was granted admission to the clubby world of professional sports ownership, the Leafs instantly became the best-capitalized ownership group in hockey. Now that Teachers' has grown its portfolio to $88 billion, it is the wealthiest majority owner organization in all of sports. How wealthy? Paul Allen, Bill Gates's high-school buddy, owns the NFL's Seattle Seahawks and the Portland Trail Blazers of the NBA. But he is worth only $10.5 billion making him the world's thiry-second richest person, according to *Forbes*. Roman Abramovich, who has his money in Premier League soccer club Chelsea, is fifty-first on the *Forbes* list with a net worth of $8.5 billion.

Though he is loath to take the credit, much of Teachers' success is due to Lamoureux. When he retired as CEO in 2007, he had turned a staid pension plan that was failing to keep pace with the requirements of its members into the most dynamic of its breed. "They have really set trends and broken new ground with respect to how these organizations need to be run," says Keith Ambachtsheer, director of the Rotman School of Pension Management at University of Toronto. Then again, Lamoureux had no choice but to break new ground. Founded in 1917, Teachers' was an agency of the Ontario government, matching contributions from the province's educators and investing them in non-negotiable provincial bonds to ensure teachers' retirements. It was boring, but it worked reasonably well. At least until 1975, when the teachers' unions negotiated the right to have their benefits indexed to the cost of living. In an era of soaring inflation, it was an understandable demand, but by 1989 the plan was under-funded by 25 percent, leaving more than 300,000 teachers with uncertain futures.

The solution was nearly revolutionary: privatize the fund's management and provide them the latitude to make investments that carried some risk, yes, but also a greater chance at a return that could allow the fund to meet its obligations. Lamoureux was trained as an actuary—someone who calculates risk—who rose to become CEO of insurance giant Metropolitan Life's Canadian operations. He was recruited to his new job by Gerald Bouey, the former governor of the Bank of Canada and the first chairman of the Ontario Teachers' Pension Plan Board when the province set it up as an independent corporation. Skeptical at first, Lamoureux turned down the job initially, doubting that he'd be given the opportunity to do what he wanted to do as CEO. "From day one we wanted to run it like a business," recalls Lamoureux. "I knew how to run a business. I hire, I fire. You don't perform, you're out of a job. You're held accountable. And Gerald delivered everything he said he would."

Lamoureux delivered on his end too, growing the fund by an average of 11.4 percent annually. About $25 billion of the fund's assets were directly attributable to the investment strategy Lamoureux implemented. He did it by harnessing an approach never before seen in the industry, leaving the world of bonds and guaranteed investment certificates behind and essentially becoming Canada's largest investment bank. Cautious and boring were left behind. Lamoureux and Bob Bertram, Teachers' chief investment officer, rapidly moved into commodities, junk bonds, quantitative investing, emerging markets and private equity. Figuring the fund needed more real estate in their asset mix, they didn't simply buy some land. They bought Cadillac Fairview, spending $2.3 billion to become one of Canada's biggest commercial landlords, with flagship holdings such as the Toronto Eaton Centre, Vancouver's Pacific Centre and the iconic Toronto-Dominion Centre office tower complex. By the same token, they concluded they needed exposure to sports and entertainment in their portfolio, which was handy because Stavro needed a backer to fund his takeover bid for Maple Leaf Gardens in the confusing years after the death of Harold Ballard.

Having sports in your portfolio is not the same as being a fan. The deal, finalized in May 1994, was put together by George Engman, the original head of Teachers' private-equity portfolio. Upon returning to the Teachers' offices to announce the transaction, one of his staff, a Montrealer, had a wisecrack ready. "We bought the Leafs?" he deadpanned. "We should have bought the Habs. We should have bought a real hockey team."

To which Engman replied, quizzically, "What are the Habs?"

And so began Teachers' passionate romance with NHL hockey.

When the deal was announced publicly, there was no talk about dreams come true or championships on the near horizon. Quite the opposite. In a brief that appeared in *Pension and Investment,* an industry publication (without a sports section), the move was described with rapturous enthusiasm. "As part of fulfilling a target allocation of 2 percent to 3 percent of the portfolio over the next seven years, the fund's internal investment team is concentrating on several industries, particularly the entertainment industry," said Bertram, senior vice-president of investments. "We don't see our investment as a hockey team purchase. We're buying into a good entertainment company. . . . While there is some risk in the investment, overall we're confident that this investment will end up being one of our better earners." He was right, of course. Spectacularly right.

At the peak of the market in late 2007, MLSE's internal evaluation suggested the organization was worth $1.7 billion. What had been a hockey team in a tired old arena became a company that included the Air Canada Centre, still one of the leading arenas of its kind more than a decade after opening, and the Toronto Raptors, an NBA franchise that has consistently ranking among the top ten revenue-producing teams in the sport. The organization's Major League Soccer team, Toronto FC, has regularly sold out, despite winning just fifteen games over its first two seasons. It cost the organization $18 million, but Richard Peddie has estimated the team was worth as much as $80 million by 2008.

If that sounds like a lot of money, keep in mind that the Leafs raked in nearly that much in ticket revenue alone in 2007–08 ($78 million). Then add in $35 million (US) more for television, radio and merchandise sales, and more still for sundries like the beer (and burgers) sold at the rink and the luxury suites themselves, and you begin to see why the Leafs are the most valuable franchise in the NHL. And a great investment.

The proper response for a hockey fan is, "Who cares?" The reason Leaf fans are Leaf fans has nothing to do with the investment returns Teachers' or any other members of the ownership group enjoy each year. Fans make investments, too, with their money and their time. So the billion-dollar question for Teachers' is not whether the Leafs and MLSE are the best investment for them, but whether they are the ownership group best positioned to bring fans a return on their investment: a Stanley Cup, or even a whiff of one.

Even those close to the plan doubt it. "I think the teams would be better served with an entrepreneurial owner that is passionate about winning and might be willing to spend way over budget to do it. Some moves might not make sense from a strict business point of view," said one high-ranking Bay Street source with close ties to the Teachers' board. "It's hard for a fiduciary to justify spending an extra $50 million that would otherwise flow to the bottom line. An entrepreneur can roll the dice to try and win a championship, but Teachers' has to think about their clients."

🍁

JIM DEVELLANO WAS WONDERING what was on Mike Ilitch's mind when he was summoned to the Detroit Red Wings' owner's office in the summer of 1985. Devellano was a respected hockey executive with three Stanley Cup rings to his credit thanks to his contributions to building the New York Islanders dynasty in the early 1980s. It was that background that put him high on the list of potential general managers when Ilitch, who had turned a small pizza business into a fortune worth billions, bought the Wings in 1982.

The club had been in the Norris family since 1932, but the legend of Hockeytown was running on fumes. Gordie Howe hadn't lifted the Stanley Cup overhead since 1955. The Dead Things, as the team had become known, had made the playoffs once in the previous eighteen years. It was a case of benign neglect, and Ilitch was able to take the once-proud franchise off the Norrises' hands for $3 million and three Chuck E. Cheese franchises, which, it was argued by some at the time, had a better chance at making the playoffs.

As the Brian Burke of his day, Devellano was the hot general-manager prospect, having learned his trade alongside Bill Torrey with the Islanders. Ilitch signed Devellano to a deal worth $375,000 over four years, with only half of the final year guaranteed. Ilitch closed the deal after touring Devellano around suburban Detroit for two days, before finally coming to an agreement over a coffee at the Detroit International Airport, having driven his new GM there himself.

Ilitch's personal touch was never far away, Devellano would realize. And his owner was every bit as competitive as any of his players. When he summoned Devellano to his office in the summer of 1985, the Red Wings had made some progress in the previous three seasons and were coming off consecutive playoff appearances (albeit first-round exits) for the first time in eighteen years. A kid named Steve Yzerman, drafted fourth overall in 1983, was emerging as a star. The farm system was growing in depth. But Ilitch wasn't satisfied. Long before Brian Burke was sniffing around college campuses trying to add to the Leafs' organizational depth, the Red Wings were doing it in a big way. "Jimmy, how many good college free agents are there out there?" he demanded. It was a revealing question. Undrafted US college players were one of the few sources of free-agent talent teams could tap. So Ilitch's question indicated an owner who knew a thing or two about adding assets to his team.

When Devellano returned from a meeting with his

hockey staff with the answer—they thought there were seven potential NHL players available in the college system—Ilitch's instructions were clear: Sign them all. Even Devellano was shocked. "Mr. Ilitch, there are twenty other clubs bidding for these players. If you want me to sign all of them, we're really, really going to have to outbid twenty other teams."

"I will never forget his answer," says Devellano in his memoir, *The Road to Hockeytown,* "because it was pretty clear and really demonstrated what a keen competitor he was, and that he was prepared to do anything to bring a winner to Detroit."

"I don't care," Ilitch said. "Sign them all."

Of the seven free agents the Red Wings scouting department identified as possible NHLers, Devellano was able to sign five, among them a Toronto-area prospect named Adam Oates. That Oates was dealt to St. Louis before his prime—"It's not one of the trades I'm proud of," says Devellano—doesn't diminish the obvious genius of the signing spree. Oates now resides in sixth place on the NHL's all-time assists list. And the other owners were threatened enough by Ilitch's aggression that the following year the league instituted a supplemental draft designed to ensure a more egalitarian distribution of free agents who'd been passed up in the entry draft.

To this day Devellano calls the supplemental draft, which was held from 1986 to 1994, "the Mike Ilitch draft."

It is one anecdote among many that shows the impact Ilitch had on an organization that was a crumbling mess when he took it over. And while the Red Wings' fantastic financial growth over his ownership tenure has allowed him to take financial risks other owners might not, that's only part of the story behind Ilitch's willingness to sign cheques if doing so will win championships. Given that the franchise was valued at $303 million by *Forbes* in 2008, Ilitch and his family have done well in the hockey business. But when he was summoning his general manager to his office and demanding he sign every available free agent, he was the owner of a team dying on the vine with a season-ticket base of just 2,000.

So consider the message Devellano sent to his team and the entire hockey community when he handed each member of the Red Wings an envelope as they walked in the front door of Ilitch's palatial home for the end-of-season party following Detroit's unexpected run to the conference finals in 1986–87, a run made possible when they came back from a 3–1 hole in the second round against a terrible Leafs team anchored by Wendel Clark. A matchup against Wayne Gretzky and the emerging Oilers dynasty in the next round ended the Red Wings' surprising surge from 40-point cellar-dwellers the year before to one of hockey's feel-good stories that season.

Being beaten by the firewagon Oilers was hardly the most humiliating way to go out, and Ilitch liked the direction the team was heading in. So he ended the campaign on a high note by handing each player an envelope filled with $13,500 in cash, doubling the NHL bonus the team earned for making the final four. Devellano, entering the final year of his contract, was given an envelope containing a three-year contract and a blank space where the salary was supposed to be, allowing the GM to name his price. Winning was expected, but it was also rewarded.

A few years later, when the Wings had become regular contenders for a Stanley Cup but were unable to break through, Ilitch stood in front of a meeting of his hockey operations staff and asked each department to come back in a week with a wish list detailing what it would take for Detroit to finally make the leap from contender to champion. When Ilitch reconvened with his hockey staff, he spoke a single word: "Well?"

The assembled hockey men had their shopping list ready, and it wasn't modest. It was suggested that flying on a charter jet to games against Western Conference opponents—not yet standard in pro sports—would ease the grind of travel. Someone else made the case that more money for free agents would help the cause. They wanted more scouts. They wanted a nutritionist and a masseuse.

The Red Wings owner nodded and said: "You've got them all. But now it's on you."

In just a few minutes, all the chips were on the table. Money and jobs were now at stake. But it all paid off in

1996–97, when the Wings won the first of the four Cups they would hoist over the next twelve seasons.

✦

IT'S HARD TO IMAGINE Claude Lamoureux swaggering into a meeting with Pat Quinn or John Ferguson or Cliff Fletcher or Mike Smith or—well, just about any hockey guy. That's part of the problem, isn't it? While Ilitch's big spending makes for good copy, Red Wings watchers are impressed as much by the patience and faith he has displayed in his hockey operations people as by the demands he has put on them. "The first thing people have to know is that there is one owner of the Detroit Red Wings, and that's Mike and Marian Ilitch," says Devellano, who still gets up every day and goes to work for the Wings, only now he is senior vice-president. "They bought it and hired me to be their first general manager and I'm still here, working for them. [Current general manager] Ken Holland was a minor-league goalie for us when I hired him and he's still here today. The very first player I drafted in 1983 was Steve Yzerman. We got him fourth overall because the team was lousy and he became a superstar, but he's still with us today. In Toronto you haven't had that continuity of ownership, and if you don't have continuity of ownership you end up having a lot of GMs. And that's means you have a lot of different scouts. No one gets to implement their plan." And by the way, a vice-president of hockey operations for

Detroit, Yzerman is one of the hottest executive prospects in hockey, and one more guy the Leafs never interviewed for the job they handed to Brian Burke.

To be fair, it's not like Teachers' is a bad owner. Professional sport is full of those. Owning a sports franchise seems to bring out the crazy side of otherwise rational men. Sometimes they run their teams with more passion than brains and go broke doing it. Prior to the lockout and the salary cap era, Teachers' was suitably free-spending. You could say what you liked about the Leafs, but they always had one of the biggest payrolls in the league. And investors were rewarded with their fair share of additional revenue from playoff games. What Teachers' lacks is not a bankroll. What it lacks, by definition, is the kind of vision that comes from passion, that allows for risk because the payoff isn't merely in dollars but in the thrill of victory and in civic pride. Corporate actuaries don't calculate that when they tally up risk.

Consider the case of Ted Leonsis, who survived a 1983 plane crash and responded by sitting down and writing a list of the 101 things he wanted to do in his "new" life. "Own a professional sports franchise" was an item he ticked off in 1999 when he bought the Washington Capitals. After spending most of his career navigating the tricky waters of public finance, where "executives in public companies talk about being slaves to next quarter's numbers, where you can't invest in the long term because Wall Street and shareholders want returns right now," he loved occupying the owner's chair. It was his team. He could do it his way.

Initially, he tried a spend-to-win strategy, epitomized when he traded for Jaromir Jagr prior to the 2001–02 season and gave the former Penguins star a seven-year, $77-million contract. It earned him nothing but a pair of middle-of-the-pack regular seasons in 2001–02 and 2002–03 and a first-round loss to the Tampa Bay Lightning in the 2003–04 playoffs.

Leonsis wasn't against spending money, but he was opposed to spending money for mediocre results. So he had a think. "I own the Capitals," he says. "It's really a public trust owned by our city. And what is the deliverable that we owe our fans? In business it might be dividends on the stock, or stock appreciation or profits. What is the deliverable that we owe our fan base, for our stakeholders? (In conversation Leonsis raises many of his own questions, and answers them. He's an easy interview.)

"What we're missing is a Stanley Cup championship. That has to be what we're all about. We can only have one big, audacious goal as an organization, and that's the missing piece. We've never won a Cup in Washington."

Leonsis was encouraged by this epiphany. You can't do what you want unless you know what you want.

"Once you come to that glaring enlightenment, you have some decisions to make. Is good enough good enough? Fighting for a playoff spot? Losing in the first round one year, maybe another year you get a hot goalie and get lucky and get a nice run. Is that good enough? Or do you tell the fans the goal is to build a generationally great team? The goal is to have a chance to win the Stanley Cup, and to do that we have to get really bad to get really good. That's really high-risk. But it's not a public company. It's a private company. And if your deliverable is to try and win a Stanley Cup, how else are you going to do it? When I say it was high-risk, I'm being sincere. There was no other choice for us. We would have wallowed as the tenth- to fifteenth-best team in the league and picked tenth or fifteenth every year and reinforced that position. So we decided we're not going to do that."

Put simply, they decided to tank. The Capitals auctioned off all their veteran talent, seeking prospects or draft picks in return. They bottomed out in the standings, finishing last in their division two straight years, improving their draft position along the way. The bounce-back came fast and quick. In 2004 they caught a break, won the NHL's draft lottery and picked Alexander Ovechkin first overall. But they also picked high-scoring defenceman Mike Green twenty-eighth. In 2006 they picked Nicklas Backstrom with the number-four pick, and he has since scored nearly a point a game, primarily as Ovechkin's linemate. The Capitals are one of the most exciting young teams in the NHL. And they are Ted Leonsis's team. Another item on his bucket list, by the way? Win a championship in a major sport.

✤

WHY, DURING THE TEACHERS' ERA, haven't Lamoureux or Bob Bertram or Jim Leech or Erol Uzumeri, who manages Teachers' Private Capital, the division within the OTPP that holds MLSE, rolled into the Leafs' hockey operations office and given them a blank cheque and set of simple instructions like "Win a Stanley Cup, no excuses," as Mike Ilitch did? Or, alternatively, why has no one said, "Let's tank and tank hard, because the only way we're going to assemble championship talent in the salary-cap era is by drafting high and well?" Ted Leonsis did it and risked plummeting attendance along the way. Teachers' has not. Why not either shoot for the top, or aim for the bottom? It's hard to know why, exactly, because the sitting executives at Teachers' refused to be interviewed for this book.

So let's be generous. Why do the people who run Teachers' do what they do? Because they're good at their jobs. They have a responsibility to their constituents and act accordingly. Hardly a scandalous idea. Getting swept up in the moment is the antithesis of their role. Sure, they want to win, but that's not the point. "The two guys I was closest to were Claude and Bob. I know them very well," says Keith Ambachtsheer, the pension expert. "And I've seen them at games. They get excited, just like everyone else, but they are very good at managing their excitement. Once they're back in the boardroom it's all about the investment doing what it is supposed to be doing from the point of view of Teachers.' That's their primary fiduciary responsibility and they do that very well. It has been a profitable investment of course, despite the losing ways of the hockey team."

Even in retirement, Lamoureux is bothered by the notion that the Leafs' playoff failures since Teachers' became owners in 1994 have anything to do with their ownership. He believes Teachers' has served Leafs Nation well, and he gets his hackles up when the suggestion is made otherwise. "People would criticize us for not spending enough. [Before the lockout] we paid twice what Calgary, Edmonton and other teams were paying. I don't want to insult sports journalists, but I would read the stories and say, gosh, these guys are weak in math." It's a line delivered playfully, rather than with intent to insult, but he makes his point.

"We are proud. No one here, nobody, no one, wants to lose in hockey or anything. Every investment we make. And in this case, eventually, it's more than an investment. You want your team to win. I told you, teachers, what do they talk about? What are the Leafs doing? Board members, during the hockey season, and even with basketball, 'Hey, how are the Raptors?' I would say half the conversation would be on the Leafs and half would be on every other investment we have—this is outside the boardroom. Our interest is the same as any owner. I am convinced of that."

And no one can accuse the Teachers' executives of being indifferent to the glamour of owning one of the world's most prestigious sports franchises. Not many people get their own bobblehead in a Leafs sweater, but Claude Lamoureux did; the tables at his retirement party were decorated with the things, each inscribed with words that resonate warmly in every Canadian's heart: "The First Star, La Première Étoile." Don Cherry himself paid tribute by video. Though MLSE is supposedly just one investment among many for Teachers', and hardly a massive one at that, that's not the way it looks sometimes. "There is a view that [OTPP executives] fell in love with the asset," says a Bay Street source close to the Teachers' board. "It's very unusual that three of the top executives sit on the board of one company. Be it a hockey team or a widget factory, you're not supposed to fall in love with the assets."

We believe Lamoureux when he says Teachers' wants to win a Stanley Cup. But though you might be able to take the man out of actuarial science, you can't take the actuarial science out of the man. No surprise then that his favourite sports book is *Moneyball* by Michael Lewis. Part biography, part evocation of the fascination baseball holds for so many fans, part a hymn to the mysteries of statistics, Lewis's classic is a brilliantly reported explanation about how Oakland Athletics general manager Billy Beane squeezed winning season after winning season from a roster built out of bargain-basement players. If you don't like the idea that sport is a business, don't read *Moneyball*.

"It's a great book," says Lamoureux. "A fabulous book. The guy didn't have the money, so he has to use his brain." It's the kind of discussion Lamoureux can relate to better than just about anyone else. After all, he's a numbers guy with one eye on the spreadsheet and the other on the scoreboard. If a franchise can win *and* save money, he's all for it.

The Oakland Athletics, however, haven't won a World Series since 1989, back in the final year of Beane's short and unaccomplished major league career, when the future general manager was hitting .241. And for all his success wringing regular-season victories out of a discount payroll, Beane's playoff record as general manager is not a whole lot better than his batting average as a player. The A's have qualified for the American League Championship Series only once under his stewardship, in 2006. When they were swept by Mike Ilitch's Detroit Tigers.

Yes, *that* Mike Ilitch. After buying the franchise in 1992, the Red Wings' owner watched it flounder until he could take it no more. He appointed himself team president in 2001, and launched a quick and painful makeover that took the club to the brink of a championship in five years. It 2003, the Tigers went 43–119, recording the most losses in American League history. In 2006 they were playing in the World Series.

Owners matter. It's easy to believe Peddie when he says that the board has never refused a request from the hockey operations. But sometimes it's up to the boss to do the asking. There are two franchises in Detroit that would still be near the bottom of their leagues if it weren't for one guy.

You don't have to make the case that the managers at Teachers' don't care about the Leafs to argue that they are hurting the team. You just have to point out that they don't care *enough*. They don't care as much as the owners who make winning personal. And if you're not committed to the boardroom equivalent of leaving it all on the ice, the odds are not great. "If you just go by random probability, you're going to win one year out of thirty. But if I'm decent at probability, I have to tell you, if everything is equal, it's easy to see you might win one in fifty years," said Lamoureux. "It's amazing, when you have thirty teams, there is only one that is going to win."

Tell that to the Red Wings.

THE LEAFS DO IT AGAIN

MARCH 5, 1988: A 10–1 loss to the Winnipeg Jets before 16,382 at Maple Leaf Gardens. Goalie Ken

Wregget is booed by the home crowd, but the
Leafs are outshot 50–18.

NOVEMBER 7, 1988: The Leafs trade Russ Courtnall to
the Montreal Canadiens for John Kordic and a
sixth-round pick who becomes Mike Doers.
Courtnall goes on to be an NHL All-Star and
represent another maple leaf at the Canada Cup.

NOVEMBER 27, 1988: During a 6–3 loss to the lowly
Minnesota North Stars, Harold Ballard angrily
abandons his Maple Leaf Gardens bunker in the
third period after Curt Giles scores for the vis-
itors from centre ice. "It's a disgrace," says GM
Gord Stellick.

Another heartbreaking overtime loss in the playoffs? Don't think so; this poor guy wasn't photographed in black and white.

Chapter Eight
Blame the Fans

"Everyone is envious of the religion called the Toronto Maple Leafs."

–*Paul Godfrey, then-president of Toronto Blue Jays baseball club, on the lucrative loyalty of the fans of Toronto's NHL team*

IT'S FIVE MINUTES TO SIX—show time—and Daren Millard, the upbeat host of Sportsnet Ontario's *Hockey Central* panel asks Bill Watters, "Who did you have on today?" Between them is Nick Kypreos, who has expertly made the transition from retired player to edgy commentator, his elegantly scarred mug in many ways the face of the network. The three of them are settling into their chairs in the glass-and-steel set in the new Rogers "campus" on Jarvis Street. The gleaming desk, the banks of television screens, the tidy sheaves of notes: this looks like the kind of place where important things are discussed and debated.

Millard is looking for trouble. Watters is the host of

Leafs Lunch on AM 640, and also hosts the station's Leafs-centric afternoon drive show that dares to compete with another institution, Bob McCown's *Prime Time Sports* on The Fan 590. Millard—who goes by "Mallard," as in duck, naturally—is the host of *Hockey Central at Noon* on The Fan. "I talked to Bryan Murray and Gerber," says the curmudgeonly Watters. Considering the woeful Ottawa Senators had just announced that they were sending struggling goalie Martin Gerber down to the team's AHL affiliate in Binghamton, New York, getting the goalie and the Ottawa GM on the show is a decent day's effort (Gerber's washout in Ottawa didn't stop the Leafs from adding him to their own roster at the 2009 trade deadline). "Really?" says Millard. "We had some reporter from Phoenix who knew less about what was going on there than we did."

"Wow," says Kypreos. "Mallard, they kicked your ass," thus setting the tone for another night at the office, where the three men carry on roughly like a trio of amiably grumpy buddies trapped in an endless loop of bad Leafs games and verbal sparring, emerging every once in a while to communicate to the fellow members of their tribe. Little wonder the panel has been a hit for the network.

Moments later, Brad Fay, host of Sportsnet's flagship *Connected* news program, throws to Millard and the panel from main studio for the first of two hits during the news hour, and the real work begins. Between them, Kypreos,

Watters—a former player agent who spent twelve years as a Leafs executive before being ousted in 2003—and Millard, a Manitoba boy raised on the Winnipeg Jets, spend their entire working week talking hockey. And most of that time is spent talking Leafs. "On the radio we try to limit it to 30 percent Leafs, but we make sure we do it off the top or people will switch," says Millard. "The rest of the time? It's probably 80 percent Leafs."

It's not as easy as it sounds. On this night, the first night of NHL hockey following the all-star break, the task is to make relevant the Leafs' first game in three seasons against the Minnesota Wild. The Wild are perhaps the most anonymous team in the NHL, devoid of stars and dedicated to a numbing, trapping style espoused by then head coach Jacques Lemaire. And even though they're tooth-and-nail to crack the Western Conference playoff picture, they're way better than Toronto, who lost seven of eight prior to the break. "Sometimes you get sick of trying to come up with a new angle instead of spinning an old one," says Kypreos, who kills time during commercial breaks playing Brickbreaker on his BlackBerry. "Hence we end up talking about Dominic Moore."

Tonight they catch a break. Justin Pogge, the Leafs' goalie of the future—or quite possibly, not—has been called up from the Marlies for his second start with the Leafs. Good move? Bad move? How will the team respond? What will this do for the kid's confidence? Has he earned this shot? Should he be considered for the backup role next season? Did Ferguson make the right call when he figured Pogge for the goalie of the future rather than Tuukka Rask? The questions take on the urgency of a G20 economic summit. Pogge's call-up is a welcome respite in a season short on storylines that don't involve Luke Schenn playing with surprising poise, Mike Van Ryn getting hurt, Vesa Toskala letting in one goal too many, or Ron Wilson benching a guy who played a lot of minutes for his predecessor Paul Maurice. "We should send Brian Burke a thank-you card for bringing up Pogge," says Millard. "At least we have something to talk about."

The reality is, it hardly matters. The Leafs could call up Donald Duck to play goalie—and hey, he might not do much worse than Pogge, who is drilled for six goals on twenty-one shots by the Wild—and Leaf fans would tune in. As the sun rises, so do the citizens of Leafs Nation gather around the flickering embers of their hockey team.

And that, more than anything, is what makes the team such a great investment. Just ask the investors. Jim Leech, chief executive officer of Teachers', knows this clients' money is in the right place because he was on hand to witness what happened to the hockey team in the 1980s. He watched as the Leafs posted thirteen straight losing seasons and still packed the Gardens for every home game. "The Leafs are the Leafs," he says in an earlier interview. "I've never seen a brand that is so resilient, and I mean that. When I came to the city in 1979 it was awful, what was going on. Everything that you could think of to try and damage it was done. But the second game of the first round of the playoffs, I'm kept awake at night in my house because everyone's honking two hours after the game's over. It's amazing. I've never seen anything like it. That level of passion gives you confidence, for sure. It's remarkable. It blows my mind." If that blind devotion gets noisy enough to keep a pension-fund manager awake every once in a while, well, that's just fine. It allows him sweet dreams on most nights.

And not just Leech. Canada's three 24-hour sports networks are banking on Leaf fans tuning in to get their fix. Not to mention the venerable CBC and its flagship *Hockey Night in Canada*. Or those bastions of Leafs Nation, The Fan 590 and AM 640, the latter of which tried to steal some of The Fan's market share by paying about $2 million a year for the radio broadcast rights to the Leafs and building much of their programming around Leafs content.

Want an audience? Talk about the Leafs. Want to sell something? Put the famous blue-and-white crest on it. Sure, all the parties involved, from Teachers' down to Nelson Millman, the long-time program director at The Fan, would love to bask in the upside of a Leafs Stanley Cup. Like a wedding or Christmas, there's no doubt people would dig in their pockets to celebrate the occasion. But the real secret of the Leafs is that the fans will keep watching, and the money keep rolling in, no matter the results.

You want to know why your favourite hockey team is a success even though the goaltender choices on any given night are Vesa Toskala, Curtis Joseph, Justin Pogge or Martin Gerber? Even though half the lineup could probably clear waivers on any given day? Why the most exciting story in an entire season is a teenage defenceman who had two goals, 12 assists and was minus-12?

Blame the fans. Blame yourself.

🍁

THE QUESTION IS, can love hurt?

Twenty miles from the Rogers studio, Julian Sanchez is settling into his couch, waiting for his Leafs to hit the ice. The setting is like a wet dream shared by Mike Myers's Wayne Campbell and Richard Peddie. His television is framed by a Wendel Clark bobblehead on one side and a Carlton the Bear bobblehead on the other. A signed Clark jersey is draped over the coffee table. And no, no one puts coffee anywhere near it. At twenty-five years old, it goes without saying that Sanchez has never seen a Stanley Cup parade. But still, he waits and he watches. Not always without complaint, but he watches. Every game.

"It really comes down to what you consider a fan," he says. "My definition of being a fan is you follow your team in good times and bad times. Sure, right now it's pretty dire, but before lockout the Leafs made the conference finals four times in twelve years. That's a lot of success in a sport that that often comes down to a bad bounce or a lucky break. I don't know what people expect. Should you be a fan only if they expect to win a championship?"

Sanchez not only watches the Leafs, he consumes them. And then—early in the morning, before heading to work as an economic development officer with the City of Mississauga, or on stolen moments at lunch—he manufactures a unique brand of content for like-minded obsessives who simply can't get enough Leafs in their lives. "Pension Plan Puppets" is the name of the blog he started in the summer of 2006 with a friend named Jason Orach. Does love hurt? Observe the unique brand of self-loathing that comes with worshipping a team that doesn't win and makes a lot of money doing it—have a look a the limp goalie dangling from marionette strings on the blog's main page. "It's a labour of love," Sanchez says. "And hate."

It's also often hilarious in the ribald, ESPN-without-a-censor tone that dominates the sports blogosphere. Its subtitle is "A Toronto Maple Leafs Blog: Blake Free in 2012!" Pension Plan Puppets is the hub of the Barilkosphere, a constellation of fellow Leaf victim blogs. Meet contributors with handles like "Loser Domi" or "Bitterleaffan." (Another, "1967er," appears to be determined to profile every Leaf to ever don the uniform; hence you get two-day stretches when Jason Podollan, who played fourteen games over two seasons in Toronto, recording two assists, is featured adjacent to Lanny McDonald, the Leafs legend who scored 219 of his 500 NHL goals during his seven seasons in Toronto.) On the main page, John Tavares updates are posted regularly and wishfully. A regular feature is the "Negative Nancy Notebook": "a daily look at how anyone, from Toronto writers to the opposition's media vultures to other bloggers, can always find a stormy cloud for any silver lining. It runs after every (usually) Leafs game and tries to highlight the bad in case anyone started to feel too good about the Leafs. Right now it's pretty easy to write. Someday soon we hope that it'll be a bit harder." A late-January post was titled "Leaf Blowers" in reference to Toronto's penchant for giving up leads, "not the nubile coeds that would love to keep Luke Schenn awake all night."

It goes on and on. Sanchez's bio captures fifteen years of dashed hopes and pain, the scar tissue of any true fan: "I've been a fan since I could crawl," it reads. "I lived through Allan Bester's five-hole. I saw grown men cry when Gretzky scored a hat trick in THAT game 7. I drove 160 km/hr to get to a Yonge Street parade. I remained a Leafs fan even though Ottawa got a team. I spent an entire paycheque to see Game 3 against the Canes in 2002. I'll make it through these bad times and it'll make the successes that much sweeter."

So love and hate yes, but mostly love. And that's because the Leafs are not just "sports and entertainment," and certainly not a "product." Like every Leaf fan, Sanchez has a story. When his father Leonardo came to Canada from Colombia in 1974 to pursue a career in civil engineering, it was clear that his first passion, soccer, was going to go unrequited for some time. When you live in Guelph, Ontario, supporting Club Deportivo Los Millonarios back in Colombia poses its problems. Besides, there was a team in his new home that people followed with the same fervour. Becoming a Leafs fan and a hockey fan was part of the Canadian experience for Leonardo. With the possible exception of the weather, there is no better social lubricant or topic for casual conversation around the office than the trials and tribulations of the Leafs.

Leonardo was determined to learn to skate, donning blades for the first time in his mid-thirties, joining shinny games with his co-workers and playing in a local church league. And when his first son was born in 1983, Saturday nights were already scripted. "I was born into a Leaf house," says Sanchez. "Saturday nights, the game came on and we were always there watching. My sister was a Leaf fan because she was held hostage. We only had one TV. . . . Watching the Leafs was a vital way for us to feel integrated here."

So when Sanchez sits down to his keyboard, he remembers the good, not the bad. The associations forged on those long-ago Saturday nights have created a bond so strong that the blunders at the ACC, whether on the ice or in the front office, can do little to convince him to forsake the Leafs. Instead, he thinks of his first Leafs game, when he was six years old: the snacks and chocolates packed by his mother, Ligia, for the long trip by train from Cobourg, Ontario, where they eventually settled; climbing the stairs at College subway station, a stone's throw from Maple Leaf Gardens; seeing his own breath mingle with that of thousands of others as they packed into the old barn; the scalpers' cries; the mounting excitement.

When even the cynics of Leafs Nation are this sentimental, it's pretty clear that Toronto fans are not about to end their romance with their team. Nor have the Sanchezes stopped going to games. The routine is a little different today, as Julian and his father live on opposite ends of the city, but the feelings aren't much different. They meet at Union Station, grab a hot dog from a vendor, settle into their seats, usually greens, and have a few beers, father and son united by a shared passion.

Even so, something is not quite right. Being a diehard Leafs fan has its complications. Sure, the Leafs owners have a duty to the team's fans. But their bigger duty is to their shareholders, the teachers of Ontario who are relying on them for a worry-free retirement. As a commerce graduate from Queen's University, Sanchez understands this very well. The idea that his passion and his money and his eyes on commercials during broadcasts like the 6–1 thrashing by the Wild may simply be feeding the beast is not lost on him. His love for the blue and white amounts to another trickle in the endless river of cash that turn into handsome dividends for Teachers' and the TD Bank Financial Group and CTVGlobeMedia and Larry Tanenbaum, not to mention the franchise's seemingly endless equity growth.

But even thought the name of his blog might suggest a sense of his own complicity, Sanchez is ultimately in denial. Or at least he disputes the premise that he and others like him are partially to blame. In his mind, Teachers' is a fairly diligent owner. The bulk of the forty-two years and counting of Cupless misery was built up during the Ballard years, he argues. The Stavro era paid dividends, and if things have gone off the rails following the lockout, the hiring of Brian Burke suggests lessons have been learned.

"They finally reached the point where they brought in the best guy and are going to leave him alone," he says hopefully. And as for the notion that MLSE is better served poised in perpetual mediocrity, enjoying a full building and rock-solid ratings, indifferent to the benefits of actually, you know, winning, Sanchez calls bullshit. "The issue is, can Teachers' do what is necessary to win? I think their goal is to win. A Leaf Stanley Cup would make them more money than they ever imagined."

That said, it's not as though Sanchez is beyond casting blame. He knows the real culprits for the Leafs lack of urgency, and they sit in the swathes of platinum seats. "If the corporate ticket holders stopped going, if the sponsors decided that the Leafs weren't a property worth associating with, then they might feel the pinch," he says.

DAN LOGAN IS ONE OF THOSE platinum seat holders. And although it's convenient shorthand in the modern sports era to dismiss the likes of Logan as "suits"—a certain breed of "fan" who attends games not out of passion but obligation, who wouldn't go at all if the their way weren't greased by company plastic—it doesn't seem quite fair in this case. Logan is a senior partner at Torys LLP, one the Canada's most prestigious corporate law firms, with offices in the TD Waterhouse Tower, a five-minute walk from the ACC. In this sense, Logan is definitely a suit, and he's wearing one when we meet in a Torys boardroom one winter morning. Were it about a legal matter, the bill would likely weigh in at about $500 an hour. But Logan is talking hockey, a subject he's happy to talk about for nothing.

He is representing the corporate fan, and what becomes clear right away is that this is not an oxymoron after all. Why would corporations take clients to Leaf games if they didn't want to watch Leaf games? If they really wanted to go to the ballet, surely they would go to the ballet. Why splash out for luxury boxes or platinum season tickets to games no one cares about?

So ingrained in Canadian culture is the right of businesses to entertain clients or potential clients at Leaf games that there's a provision for it in the Income Tax Act, outlining precisely in which circumstances a business can claim 50 percent of the value of their tickets or luxury boxes. As a courtesy, the legislation allows tickets for the other Canadian NHL team and restaurants meals and theatre tickets to be deducted as well. In any case, paragraph 67.1(4)(b) includes "amusement and recreation" as "entertainment." Section 67.1 also mentions the "enjoyment of entertainment." We're not accountants, but a strict interpretation of the tax code suggests that the events should be, you know, *fun* in order to be deductible. By that narrow definition, do the Leafs even qualify? How many millions of dollars' worth of tickets have been deducted by companies that "entertained" clients by taking them to watch bad teams? Seriously. Is this not a case for the Canada Revenue Agency? Should corporate tax files be audited to ensure that the Leafs played well enough to deserve being called "entertainment"?

If so, Torys accountants could have their work cut out for them. The firm's founder bought his first season tickets in 1931, the year the Gardens opened. They were incredible seats: the second row behind the glass, behind the goal judge. Over the years they kept adding seats, eventually bringing the total to an even dozen. Oh, and they have a box, too. It's an impressive investment. Last season alone, each of the twelve seats carried a face value of $180.43. Add in the cost of meals the Platinum Lounge—allow $100 per person—and any given contest between the Leafs and the Tampa Bay Lightning could run the firm about $3500.

Not even a global recession is enough to raise any serious discussion in the Torys boardroom about giving up the Leaf tickets. As Logan points out: "We've had these seats for a long time. It's not just that we've been through recessions with them before; we've gone through *depressions* and we still have them. Short of the world stopping turning, I can't see the firm saying this is not a worthwhile activity for our firm and for our clients."

There is something to be said for having great seats. "[The quality] of our seats does matter," says Logan. "We hear that a lot. Most of these people have been to a game, but they haven't been in seats where if you're booing because someone missed their check, they may and stop and talk with you. I don't think I've ever been there when the people I'm with haven't commented on the seats. There's a vividness to the game you don't get from the greys. You realize the nastiness and the brute strength and this whole intensity that's not obvious on TV or in the greys or the greens. It brings to it a whole component that is missing as you move further from the ice."

That's right: he's there to watch the game. From way up at the top of the ACC bowl, it might be easy to cast dagger eyes at the corporate season-ticket holders who take up the majority of the platinum seats, but up close it's harder. Cut Dan Logan and he bleeds not just blue, but blue and white. Like Julian Sanchez and his family, the Logans were once strangers in a strange land. They moved to Toronto from Montreal in the early 1970s, leaving too soon to revel in the Habs' dynasty, arriving too late for the Leafs'. As a five-year-old, he went to his first hockey tryout in Toronto wearing Maurice Richard's number 9 jersey, an infidel on an ice surface patrolled by little Davey Keons. "It was like *The Hockey Sweater,* only in reverse," says Logan. He saw the light and has been a Leafs fan ever since.

And if the curse of the corporate fan is real, it's not new. He used to go to the Gardens with his father and sat in seats owned by Dominion Securities. The enduring value of corporate seats, says Logan, is they allow people to develop relationships without talking business. "You don't have to be great at marketing to go off to a Leaf game," he says. "All you have to be is be a hockey fan."

It's not just about closing deals and wooing new accounts. Logan's favourite moments are when he can be "just" a fan, and invite clients to do the same. With twelve season tickets at his disposal, Logan has the luxury of bringing not just key clients, but their spouses and their kids, along with his family too. Suddenly it's not a bunch of heavy hitters in suits retiring to the Platinum Lounge between periods; it's a big group doing what families do, including trying to dab the ketchup stain out of Junior's Leafs jersey. "That's the high-water mark. . . . When you can provide an opportunity for your clients where they don't have to choose between work and family," says Logan. "You're not taking people away from their families. Most of the people we work with are like me and my family: they're going 100 miles an hour all the time. A night out means they have to get a sitter. The idea of doing something at night or the weekend means time away from their kids, and it's like 'Are you crazy? What do you mean we're doing a client development thing on the weekend? Are you insane?' But the minute you say we're going to the Leaf game and we're taking the kids and put on your jeans, it's 'Well, this doesn't sound too bad.'"

As for feeling complicit about aiding and abetting a franchise that hasn't won a Stanley Cup since he arrived in Toronto, yet charges his firm nearly $200 for a seat, well, actually Logan does. A little. Torys may just be paying what the market will bear for the hottest tickets in town, but the market doesn't seem to care that the average Canadian family wouldn't be able to afford them. "If taking a family and kids and having hot dogs and Cokes costs $700, that's a problem. I suspect the downward pressure [of the global recession] is forcing people to look elsewhere for other entertainment opportunities, and that's too bad," says Logan. "But at the end of the day, [the Leafs] are responsible to their share-holders, I guess, and they'll make their decisions accordingly. We shouldn't be surprised at this trend. Do I feel complicit? I feel less complicit when I'm not in the box. I'm not sure why that it is."

IT SEEMS THAT EVERYONE, from the suits in the plat-inums to the bloggers up in the bowl, really does love the Leafs. Could that ever change? Could the Leafs ever slip from their pedestal and lose their dominance in the marketplace? An MLSE survey revealed that 69 percent of Leafs Nation described themselves as "big" fans in 2006–07; that number had fallen to 51 percent the following year. The Leafs' own research is backed up by a similar finding by the US sporting giant ESPN, which ranked the Leafs 121st out of 122 professional sports teams in its fan satisfaction survey in 2008. That makes them the least satisfying team to support in the NHL, since the only team lower in the rankings was the feeble Detroit Lions of the National Football League. Ouch.

Club officials blamed the lockout, three years (now four) of losing and an increasingly diverse city as threats to a brand that has been the symbol of WASP Toronto for eight decades. And while Julian Sanchez and Dan Logan grew up watching the Leafs, today's kids may well be interested in other things. The average Toronto Raptor fan is five years younger than the average Leaf supporter.

The remedy is more practices in more neighbourhood arenas—about fifteen of which are slated to be refurbished thanks to a $1.5-million program launched by MSLE in partnership with Home Depot—and equipment drives to create opportunities for kids who can't afford to play the game. "We've been accused of taking fans for granted, and that's bull. But we certainly need to do better where our fans are concerned," says Tom Anselmi, MLSE's chief operating officer. "We want to take the team to the city, be more accessible."

Well, if there's a crisis, or even a concern, it's not apparent over at Sportsnet, where blanket Leaf coverage continues no matter how the team fares on the ice or what the club's surveys say. But then Sportsnet would probably not exist if not for the Leafs. It didn't receive its blessing from the Canadian Radio-television and Tele-communications Commisssion until it paid $15 million to the NHL for national cable rights in Canada. The network only broke through in 2002, when it spent $12 million to acquire the rights from TSN to broadcast sixty Leaf games in Ontario (scheduling conflicts with other properties made it practical for TSN to off-load some games at a profit). And Sportsnet scored another coup in 2007 when it agreed to pay $700,000 a game for local Leafs rights through the 2014–15 season.

Getting Leafs games drives all broadcast strategy, it seems. TSN paid $200 million over five years for NHL rights—as long as they could take a record seventeen

Leaf games national. The CBC spends $100 million a year on NHL rights, in part for the privilege of showing twenty-three Leaf games on Saturday night each season.

For Sportsnet, on a strict money-out, money-in perspective, showing Leaf games is a loss leader. "MLSE is in a position where they get more than one bid for their local rights," says David Akande, head of programming and news at Sportsnet. "So it's not like our bid is a break-even proposition. From advertising revenue alone, we lose money, outside our cable or affiliate revenue. But it's important to us." Sportsnet has been profitable every year since it began broadcasting Leaf games. The Leafs provide a platform for it to advertise its other programming as well as audiences that lead into its late-night sports shows, not to mention content for those shows. "On the days that we have a Leaf game, the energy is a little different," says Matt Marstrom, the twenty-eight-year-old producer of *Hockey Central Tonight*. "You know you're going to get good ratings, you know everyone is Ontario is going to be watching. Good or bad, you know people are going to tune in."

Sure enough, on this night they tune in, and in large numbers. More than 260,000 Leaf fans flick on the TV to get their first taste of the Leafs after the all-star break, to get another look at the goalie who just might be the guy to take them where Vesa, Cujo, Razor and every goalie back to Johnny Bower has failed to go. Or maybe not. What the fans got was an opening goal on a slapshot from outside the right-hand faceoff circle by Wild winger Cal Clutterbuck. Somehow the puck found the top right-hand corner of the net over Pogge's 6-foot-3 frame. At Sportsnet, Kypreos and Watters are having burgers and Greek salad ("Tell them the salad is for me," says Kypreos, who requires extra feta cheese, to one of the production assistants as he heads out for the food. "Don't let them embarrass themselves."), while Millard digs into a bulging tuna sandwich. Dinner is served in a small meeting room dominated by a massive flat screen where they watch the game when they're not in front of the cameras themselves. The goal is shown perhaps half a dozen times in slow motion. Give it to the boys at Sportsnet—they called it the first time.

"Bad goal, Wilbur," says Kypreos. "Bad goal," says Watters. Millard, a former goaltender himself, remains silent in solidarity. "He should never have been able to see the corner on that shot," says Kypreos. At home in Mississauga, Julian Sanchez is watching alone, blogging as he goes. Connecting with other Leafs fans along the way, the online comments go from cautiously optimistic to grimly suicidal by the middle of the third period. The goals pile up, the indignities too. But they don't turn it off.

THE LEAFS DO IT AGAIN

OCTOBER 23, 1999: In need of a roster spot to make room for Dmitri Khristich, acquired from the Bruins for a second-round draft pick that became Ivan Huml, the Leafs put Steve Sullivan on waivers. Sullivan is picked up gratis by the Chicago Blackhawks and goes on to register at least 60 points in seven consecutive seasons. Khristich, dumped for a third-round pick in 2001, begets Brendan Bell, who is later traded for 17 games of Yanic Perreault. Champagne follows—specifically Joel Champagne, the Leafs' selection with the fifth-round pick thrown into the Perreault deal.

APRIL 14, 2003: Named a healthy scratch for game three of a first-round playoff series with the Philadelphia Flyers, Shayne Corson leaves the Leafs. His search for solitude further divides a dressing room that was already in a serious state of rupture. The Flyers win the series in seven games.

JANUARY 15, 1986: Leafs lose 10-1 to the St. Louis Blues. "One of the all-time stinkeroos," writes Rick Fraser of the *Toronto Star.*

Red Sox Nation. Leafs Nation. Hmmm . . . We'll take the one with the giant championship banner.

Chapter Nine

Find Hope in Boston
(and, uh, not in the Bruins)

"The real answer is fire the fans. Nothing makes a hockey club get better faster than empty seats."

— *Scott Dobson, Toronto*

FANS OF THE MAPLE LEAFS have been called a lot of things. The greatest in the world. The blind following the blind. They've been faulted for being as loyal "as golden retrievers ... [a]bandoned by the side of a lonely country road, they'd sit there forever and starve to death, waiting for their master's return." (Thank you, Stephen Brunt of the *Globe and Mail*). And they've been called Leafs Nation, "Nation" being a now-ubiquitous sporting signifier first used, as best we can tell, to describe the wide-ranging fan base of the Boston Red Sox. "Red Sox Nation," as it appeared in a 1996 *Boston Globe* article, refers to the wilds of Massachusetts and Maine and Connecticut and Rhode Island and beyond—places where Boston's Major League Baseball team is the majority-preferred nine. The Leafs still enjoy a similar hold on many households in English Canada owing to their days as the only Canadian NHL team not nick-named *Les Habitants*. And until relatively recent history, of course, the fan base of the Red Sox, like that of the Leafs, was united by a decades-old run of futility.

The Curse of the Bambino, as it was known—the championship drought that followed Boston's ill-fated decision to sell the great Babe Ruth to the New York Yankees—was lifted only in 2004, after eighty-six years of frequent agony. That's when the Red Sox made an improbable run to a championship by coming back from a 3–0 series deficit against the hated Yankees to win the American League pennant in a seven-game epic before sweeping the St. Louis Cardinals to win the World Series. The Red Sox, after years of questionable management (and a legendary near-miss at the 1986 World Series that rolled through the legs of Bill Buckner), only trans-formed themselves from miserable losers to perennial championship contenders after an ownership change led to a revamping of executive ranks.

Leafs Nation isn't alone in its devotion to a peren-nial also-ran. The Chicago Blackhawks, of course, con-tinue to languish through the longest Cup-less streak in the NHL. When the Blackhawks last won the mug in 1961, Bobby Hull and Stan Mikita were their stalwarts,

and hockey players were beloved heroes in the Windy
City. In the decades that followed, the club saw its on-
ice fortunes decline as its fan base dwindled—a sad state
of affairs that could be chalked up to either the myopic
ownership of Bill Wirtz (the genius who decided it was
a good idea to black out Blackhawks games on local TV,
a move the people of Chicago responded to by forgetting they had a hockey team) or to the curse of Rudy
Pilous (the bull-headed coach of those 1961 champions
who was fired a couple of years later, in his mind unjustly,
and who noted in the last interview he ever did before
his death in 1994 that the Blackhawks "haven't won one
since, and I don't think they ever will").

Fans of the Chicago Cubs recently commemo-
rated and commiserated a century without winning a
World Series. And just as Toronto's competitive malaise
hasn't hurt the bottom line, the Cubs have been doing
just fine without holding a parade. They trade on the
beauty of their throwback ballpark, the ivy-covered
Wrigley Field, and verily revel in the team's status as a
lovable loser. Its fans have been derided for their complicity in the charade by no less a sports fanatic than
Barack Obama, an avowed supporter of the Cubs'
cross-town rival Chicago White Sox. Obama has
thumbed his nose at the Cubs' see-and-be-seen fans—
a sporting purist's criticism that rings true in Toronto,
where owners of the Air Canada Centre's platinum
seats routinely forgo large chunks of action to linger

over the luxe shrimp-and-chardonnay spreads in plush bunkers beneath.

Perhaps this is the whole problem, of course: that the people with the most spending power—the people who could, theoretically, influence the club's decision makers to improve the on-ice product by either withholding or curtailing their financial support—don't seem prepared to put their passion for the on-ice product ahead of the seats' value in doing business. They're not spending their own money in most cases; they're writing it off as a business expense. And maybe a fan base and a franchise and a city ultimately get the performance they deserve. Though the influence of corporate-seat ownership is widespread and, some would suggest, irreversible, it doesn't always breed the same kind of pulseless ennui that inhabits the Air Canada Centre on most Leafs game nights.

Witness Boston, always in the conversation as one of the best sports towns in the world, where, when the Bruins and the Celtics and the Red Sox are in action, it's sometimes easy to forget that the people in the expensive seats, many of them, are supposedly there for business purposes. It's a gross generalization and difficult to quantify, but in Boston—and in Montreal and New York and so many cities not named Toronto—there is unmistakable passion in the air on most game nights, even if Jeremy Jacobs, the owner of the Bruins for much of the past forty-five years, has tested that passion by running his team with a constant eye on spending. Jacobs runs his hockey club like it's a business above all, and that, obviously, is his right. The suits at MLSE think along the same lines. Fans are told that they should be resigned to this reality. Athletes too have the lines memorized—"It's a business"—and they deliver them with a to-hell-with-passion shrug. But people don't cheer for businesses. And clearly, the distinction doesn't have to be so clear-cut.

Consider the owners of the Celtics, the NBA franchise that, like the Leafs, saw a glorious period of success interrupted by a long stretch of ineptitude. The Celtics, in the wake of the 1980s salad days when they won three championships led by Larry Bird et al., went in some regrettable directions that left them out of the playoffs for six consecutive years at their lowest point. They hired a coach, Rick Pitino, as team president, de facto general manager and coach, and watched him all but run the team into the ground as he bungled the multiple roles.

But the rebuilding process is measured in something smaller than generations in Boston. The Celtics were back with an NBA championship in 2008, this with Pitino and the owners who hired him a distant memory. History will record that the key to that championship run was a couple of off-season deals that brought all-stars Ray Allen and Kevin Garnett into a starting lineup that already included an all-star named Paul Pierce. Less noted, but perhaps more fundamental, was the philosophy of the ownership group that took control of the team about a half-dozen years before they raised the franchise's seventeenth championship banner to the rafters.

"We are a bunch of fans who bought this team," says Wyc Grousbeck, the face of the ownership group that includes his father and a handful of partners, speaking from his office not far from the TD Banknorth Garden. "It's a we, it's a group, even though I'm the lead owner. We come at this from the fan's standpoint. We're all born and raised in Boston, or nearly, the major players, including me and my dad. So we don't know any different than being Bostonians who bought a great Boston team. But now that I've been in this six years, it's even more obvious to me that this is a business where the fan has to come first. The only way a team succeeds is if, from the courtside seat to the last seat in the balcony, everybody's on the same page, they want to support the team.

"I know that sounds kind of corny. But I happen to believe this. I will never forget raising that banner. And I will not have any idea, ten years from now, if we made money or lost money on any one of these particular years. I will not remember that. Now, that could come off like I'm some sort of multi-billionaire and that I don't care [about money]. That's actually not true. But I'll never forget raising the banner, and I will forget our financial results long before then."

Richard Peddie does not speak like this, presumably because he would be fired for speaking like this. But Grousbeck frames his involvement in sports in a way that every sports fan in the world wishes his beloved team's owner would see things. It's not just idle chatter. The Celtics spent well past the NBA's so-called luxury-tax threshold to put together their championship squad, incurring onerous financial penalties in the process, but optimistically factoring in the increases in revenue that on-court success would bring. (Meanwhile, back in Toronto, the MLSE-controlled Raptors have repeatedly stated their commitment to staying under the luxury-tax line.) Grousbeck's Celtics spent some money up front, figuring they'd make it back later. The "sports is a business" mantra doesn't have to mean that franchises should care only about money. Why shouldn't it mean that entrepreneurs have to spend money to make money? Or that the way to make money is to win?

How does this pertain to the Leafs? Certainly the NHL and NBA systems vary wildly. The NBA's salary cap is known as a "soft cap," because it allows deep-pocketed owners to outspend their foes. The NHL's is a "hard cap"—everybody has to stay under the limit and the spoils go to the smartest and the luckiest. But it's clear that an owner who is willing to spend more than his competitors can carve out an advantage in hockey's financial landscape. He can buy out bum player contracts and minimize their impact on the salary-cap ledger. He can buy out coaches and general managers who outlive their usefulness. He can spend more on scouting and development and gambling on undrafted free agents.

But he has to be willing, above all, to make decisions that aren't always sound by the standards of the business-school textbook.

This is not the mentality being instilled at MLSE. John Ferguson Jr., the general manager who managed the Leafs right out of the playoffs, was happy to take credit for running the hockey department some $10 million under budget in one of his better fiscal years. The guy may have handed out no-trade clauses like Halloween candy and shipped off enough draft picks to start a new franchise, but he knew how to save a buck here and there, which must have made someone happy enough to keep him around. But boasting that $10 million saved is $10 million earned is not exactly an entrepreneurial approach to either business *or* winning championships.

"I felt like an owner before I bought the team," says Wyc Grousbeck. "And I also feel right now like an owner of the Red Sox and the Patriots, the other teams in town, because I've been a fan as long as I can remember. Not only have I bought tickets, but I've just given my love to these teams as a Bostonian. I felt like an owner of the Celtics before I bought the Celtics, because I'd invested not just money but time and emotional energy. We are fans of this team, we bought this team, and we hold this team in trust for the fans of Boston. To someone from another city, that could sound like empty talk or a marketing spin. But to someone from Boston, who comes to the games and knows how it feels to be a

Celtics fan, I think they know that it's the truth. That's why last year was so special. It was a couple of million people winning a world championship. It's great when it works."

That's not to say it will always work. That's not to say the Celtics will be a superior franchise for all time. That's not to say Grousbeck and his group are dream owners who will do the proverbial "whatever it takes" to be victorious. It's an inexact science, and moments come and go. Windows of opportunity open and close. But the odds are that owners like Grousbeck will raise banners more frequently than owners who count the beans more precisely. And therein lies the hope for Leafs fans.

No, Grousbeck and his group aren't in the market for a hockey team. But they're setting a standard, setting an example. Teachers' will tell you everything's for sale. And maybe the next owner will understand that a sports team shouldn't be treated like just another widget factory.

"I'm not a multi-zillionaire," Grousbeck chuckles. "Don't get the wrong idea that I'm a total jerk and I'm throwing this money around. It's just not true that I have cheques lying around I haven't cashed. That stuff's not true. Did we make money [on the championship season]? Well, we could have done worse, but it wasn't our best financial year. It just wasn't. Not our best financial year, but in the long term it'll probably pay off. If you invest in a team and you get it to the top of the world, it's going to work out financially as well. But you don't have a financial statement in front of you as a road map. You have the league standings in front of you."

✤

ON NOVEMBER 22, 2008, the Air Canada Centre was looking decidedly hairy. Every member of the sellout crowd was given a kitschy souvenir of Wendel Clark's tribute night—a strawberry-blond moustache, not unlike the one Clark sported during his years in blue and white. The Leafs, every one of them, wore Clark's number 17 jersey during the pre-game warmups— jerseys that would later be autographed and used as another piece of currency by the club. The fans, who would have their moustaches to keep, would soon be pawing through the piles of Clark merchandise that had been specially prepared for sale on the evening. (A framed commemorative print could have been yours for $229!) And amid the crass commerce and legitimate emotion, forgettable words were spoken. Tears were cried. A very good career was made out to be a great one. A guy who was not quite good enough for the Hall of Fame and who never won a Stanley Cup was pampered with the kind of treatment usually reserved for sporting immortals. This is the kind of banner-raising they have to settle for in Leafland these days.

This is not to besmirch Clark, who played with a fiendish intensity that not only galvanized his team, but gave a whole city little choice but to love him. Still, it's important for a club to have standards. The Montreal Canadiens, for instance, had retired fifteen numbers by the end of the 2008–09 season. On the same night Clark was being honoured in Toronto, the Canadiens raised Patrick Roy's number 33 to the rafters of the Bell Centre. Compare the two players' careers, and you start to notice a few important differences.

Roy is a Hall-of-Famer who won four Stanley Cups and three Vezina trophies. He's the only player in history to win three Conn Smythe trophies as playoff MVP. He dominated his era. And so, his number 33 will never again be worn by a Montreal player. Or a member of the Colorado Avalanche, since that team had retired Roy's digits five seasons earlier. And Clark? While Clark was a reliable big-game player (and who will forget his hat trick in Game 6 of the '94 conference final?), he was never the best player on a Cup-contending team. Yes, he lifted his team with his physical play. And yes, he could drop the gloves with anyone in the league, most of them at least a couple dozen pounds heavier (who will forget the mess he made of Marty McSorley's face when the Los Angeles defenceman took a run at Doug Gilmour?). Clark collected 1,690 penalty minutes over the course of his career, about 1,688 of them for fighting. But as undeniably hard as he played, as laudable as that kind of spunk clearly is, Clark was as approximate a hero as a hockey team has ever had.

For this, Clark's number 17 was brought level with the eleven other supposedly "honoured" numbers in Leafland. Doug Gilmour's number 93 would follow later in the season in similar fashion, no matter that Gilmour played only four full seasons in Toronto. But at least Gilmour is a candidate for the Hall of Fame. Clark's supporters might argue he's a worthy honouree on the strength of his leadership skills. After all, it's happened before. Another Clark from Saskatchewan, Clark Gillies of Moose Jaw, comes to mind. He scored eleven fewer career goals than Wendel. But while Gillies's New York Islanders won four Stanley Cups, Number 17's Leafs won, well, none.

Why does this matter? It matters because Dave Keon, the best player from the four-Cup dynasty of the 1960s, is an actual Hall-of-Famer whose number 14 has yet to be honoured by the Leafs. While Clark's number 17 has yet to be worn again, Keon has watched a succession of relative nobodies, from Garry Monahan to Stan Weir, from Mike Kaszycki to Miroslav Frycer, from Ron Wilson to Dave Reid to Craig Laughlin to Jonas Hoglund to Rob Cimetta to Dave Tomlinson (he of the one career NHL goal) to Darby Godforsaken Hendrickson and Matt Stajan, wear his digits when they should have been hanging in the rafters. Keon is a special case, of course, an iconoclast who had an unhappy ending with the club and has continued to hold a grudge. But if there are those who suggest Keon should drop the bad feelings and embrace an Air Canada Centre celebration of his legacy, those folks fail to grasp that you don't have to be accommodating when you're right. Keon has long been a critic of the Leafs' unique practice of "honouring numbers"—almost every other heritage team in big-league pro sports retires the numbers of its great heroes, taking them out of circulation. The Leafs have never laid out a bullet-pointed defence of their practice of keeping the numbers in circulation even as they hang from the rafters—only Bill Barilko's number 5 and Ace Bailey's number 6 (along with Wayne Gretzky's number 99, which was retired around the league) are technically unavailable to current players—but they certainly can't suggest they would run out of numbers. The Montreal Canadiens, with fourteen possible jersey numbers out of circulation, don't seem to have a problem filling out a roster.

To the Canadiens, to pro sports teams with a clue, the mythology matters, and who gets mythologized matters. That there was nary a register of public outrage at the thought of immortalizing Clark's career with a banner bearing his digits and likeness—a banner that will hang alongside those of players who actually won something for the Leafs—says much. Adoring Wendel Clark won't make him a Hall-of-Famer, any more than loving the Leafs will make them Stanley Cup champions. Just the opposite. Cheer for mediocrity, and you can expect more of it.

You have to wonder how long it will take to "honour" Mats Sundin's number 13. Sure, the fans booed

Sundin frequently during his run as a talented but largely ineffectual captain. On the 2003 night when Sundin was honoured for scoring his 1,000th NHL point, Andy Frost, the announcer at the game and post-game radio host, wondered aloud to his listeners why the big Swede wasn't fully embraced by the Leaf faithful. "They just savaged the poor guy," Frost told the *Ottawa Citizen* at the time. "They said he has no heart, that's he soft, that he doesn't care about winning the Stanley Cup, that only a Canadian player can lead the Leafs to the ultimate victory. One guy said the Leafs should rip the C off his jersey and give it to [Gary] Roberts. I understand the passion, but I thought it was kind of sad, really."

The truth is, though, that Sundin had such an advanced case of Blue and White Disease that he thought he was bleeding blue and white when he refused to waive his no-trade clause in the waning days of the lost season of 2007–08. Sundin made the case to the credulous Leaf faithful that he was depriving the re-building franchise of prospects and draft picks for no reason other than the fact that he loved the team so much. Of course, he didn't love the team so much that he would have considered coming back for the next season. The Leafs lost their most prized asset to free agency, and got nothing in return.

How did the supposedly passionate Leaf fans respond to this slap in the face? How about a standing ovation? No matter that the guy had said at the trade deadline that he would never be a rental player, only to join the Canucks more than halfway through a season. No matter that in his refusal to help the Leafs he evoked all the purity of the training-camp-to-playoff journey, then sat at home when training camp started. No matter that the Canucks had almost no chance at winning a Stanley Cup and that—while Sundin insisted that his return to the league wasn't about money—the Canucks' offer was the most lucrative on the table. No matter that Sundin had essentially turned down a chance to win a Stanley Cup in the previous spring, that he'd been given the option of staying in the fight and had chosen to get out. Sundin's supporters pointed out that the captain had every right to cling to his no-trade clause, that he had earned it. Okay. Fine. But Leaf fans had every right to withhold their adoring ovation too. Sundin had not earned *that*. It's hard to imagine he would have been showered with so much inexplicable love in a more credible sports town, in a place where winning is the only thing.

But riling up Leafs Nation is no easy task. Through so many years of pathos, fan boycotts have been suggested in talk-radio ramblings, on Internet message boards, in letters to editors. "If, indeed, you wish to express your displeasure with the Leafs, you will be well advised to boycott not only their final home game, but every game," Keith Hipkins of Ridgetown, Ontario, wrote in a letter to the editor to the *Toronto*

Star in 2006. "In addition, a mass refusal to purchase anything bearing a Toronto Maple Leafs logo—posters, flags, mugs, glasses, shirts, boxer shorts, sticks, etc.—will send a clear message of displeasure directly to the franchise's coffers, since the game has become more involved with finance and profit and less involved with sport and sportsmanship."

Wrote Steve Purdey of Toronto around the same time about the depths of Ferguson's ineptitude: "The only thing we can do to express our unhappiness in a serious way is to boycott a hockey game. So let's do it. Stay away from the last game of the season at the Air Canada Centre. Bite the bullet. Tell your friends. If you're onside, let the media know it. We're the best hockey fans on the planet and we want the best team. Let's do what we need to do to get the Cup back home."

Where was the groundswell? It never showed itself.

❧

"THERE ARE FANS that are pissed off because we've lost for a few years or fans that are on the fence and we have to woo back," Tom Anselmi, the MLSE chief operating officer, told the *National Post*. "But there's also the longer term about where is the fan from tomorrow coming from." Indeed, with an estimated 100,000 new immigrants landing in the Greater Toronto Area every year, the local citizenry is, more and more, made up of people with foreign roots, sporting and otherwise.

Minor hockey isn't the force it once was, either. The Leafs used to have strategies intended to stop this kind of rot in their grassroots. As money-grubbing as the pre-MLSE regimes may have been, there was a long tradition of setting aside thousands of tickets to be sold at the box office on game days, making it possible for, say, a father and son to go to a game without forking over a week's salary to a scalper. And for many years, the Leafs gave away the use of the Gardens to various minor-hockey concerns. The Marlies minor-hockey organization—not to be confused with the current American Hockey League franchise—held many of its games and practices at the Gardens, meaning that generations of atoms and peewees and midgets had intimate connections to the big-league arena (a connection that was broken not long after some enterprising young Marlies, recognizing the notoriously lax security in the building, ransacked concession stands). And the puck enthusiasts who skated for their school teams in Toronto's public education system played a little harder in their playoff games knowing that a trip to the championship game meant they'd get to face off at the Gardens.

Still, even with soccer and basketball gaining strong toeholds—even with the waiting list for season tickets for Toronto FC sitting at about 13,000 names, far longer than the 7,500 names on the Leafs' waiting list—the Leafs are hardly in danger of being destitute anytime soon.

"We have the most loyal fans in hockey," Anselmi told the *Toronto Star* in 2008. "We've been accused in the past of taking our fans for granted, but that's crap. But we need to do a better job in our relationship with our fans. We need to improve access, have a better quality product, provide exceptional service and reward fan loyalty."

You could argue with the part about taking the fans for granted, of course, or point out that having loyal fans is not the same as having happy fans. But MLSE seemed to have figured out that they have to do *something* as the Leafs embarked on a 2008–09 season that didn't promise much (and lived down to every expectation magnificently). So they rolled out the "access" Anselmi believed they wanted. To that end, the team built a replica dressing room in the modified semi-trailer that made road trips to communities around Ontario. It invited thousands of screaming school kids to watch game-day skates from the platinum and gold seats that most of their parents presumably cannot afford. And it held the so-called "Fans First Game," a preseason tilt against the Buffalo Sabres for which all 19,000 or so tickets were said to be distributed free.

It seemed like a wonderful gift to the loyalists from the Bay Street Scrooges. Although whether it was actually a gift to the fans depends on whether your definition of "gift" includes something the giver doesn't actually pay for. Coca-Cola picked up the tab for the evening in exchange for blanket advertising and title sponsorship.

One reader's comment in the *Toronto Star*'s website skewered the whole idea: "This is just weak marketing BS. Between the money sponsored by Coke and the money from concessions etc this is costing them absolutely nothing. They will still make money off this game, guarantee every seat full and come out looking like they are doing something for the fans. If they really wanted to do something for the fans bring in real hockey people and let them have the control they need to ice a proper team. This is just more smoke and mirrors because the current ownership thinks they are a hell of a lot smarter than anyone else out there and that we are all too stupid to see through their crap." Still, the very thought of the concept—a free Leafs game!—seemed fantastical to anyone in the city without an expense account. Leafs games have become luxury items as unattainable to the regular folks as business-class plane tickets and fur coats. And sure enough, the club claimed to have received some 60,000 applications for the ticket lottery.

But when the night arrived, when Peddie took his usual seat in the platinums, something wasn't right. The club seemed to have taken every detail into consideration. The players took the ice for their pre-game warm-up in identical jerseys, all of them emblazoned with the number 1 and the words "LEAF FANS" between their shoulder blades. And the fans were given white T-shirts bearing the Leafs' new corporate slogan—"Spirit Is

Everything!" (Vince Lombardi, the late NFL coaching legend who once famously declared that "Winning isn't everything; it's the only thing," must surely have vomited in his grave.)

Alas, despite the fair ticket price, the building wasn't really brimming with foam-mouthed fanatics who'd been waiting since the 1980s to see the Leafs up close. In fact, the building wasn't even full. As the rock singer Danny Greaves sang "O Canada," Peddie could be observed swivelling in his seat to take a head count. What he saw was a patchwork of thousands of empty seats. They came in every colour: platinums, golds, reds and blues. It must have been difficult to figure out. Wasn't this the club that had been so derided for charging the highest ticket prices in hockey for so many seasons? Wasn't this the night in which the fans could finally claim to be paying exactly what the product has been worth on so many nights?

Peddie, who stopped for a chat with a reporter during a first-intermission jaunt to the directors' lounge, claimed not to be surprised by the turnout. Though the club could announce a crowd of 18,819—in other words, a full house—Peddie acknowledged that the turnstile count was a little different. He estimated the crowd at 85 percent of capacity, or about 16,000. Which meant that, on a night when the supposed hottest ticket in town was available for nothing, nearly 3,000 of the ducats went unused.

There was some evidence that ticket speculators got a little overzealous in trying to turn the free tickets into a profit. In the lead-up to the game, Internet buy-and-sell sites had no end of nervy entrepreneurs trying to fleece Leafs Nation. (Some guy on Craigslist wanted $300 for a pair of golds. And scalpers outside the arena were answering the time-honoured question, "How much?" with the ancient response, specifically, "How much do you want to pay?")

That's not to say that a good time was not had by all who came. The platinum seats, usually the domain of the dry-clean-only set, had probably never seen so many hard-cores in machine-wash replica jerseys bearing the names of local heroes, from Tucker to Roberts to Sundin. The Leafs won in a walk, 7–4. And for an exhibition game, it was a relative trip. Wendel Clark presented one lucky attendee with a year's supply of pop. Another fan went home with a pair of season tickets. But the free game was not the free-for-all some figured it would be. The white T-shirts were not donned en masse to create a Winnipeg-style white-out, as the proprietors had hoped. And this distinct lack of fervour was not lost on anyone—least of all the man in the front row in the blue-and-white clown wig.

"People are complaining about ticket prices being so high. Then they give 'em away, and it's not full," said Kyle Mungar, a Hamilton landscaper who sat by the glass in face paint and the wig. "I think the fans are a little bit nervous because it's a whole new team this year. Everyone's like 'Leafs suck' because they're starting from fresh right now. But I'm surprised it's not packed to the top. My friends were going to come with me, but they thought it would be too packed. . . . I don't understand it."

Peddie, never to be stumped, said he understood it.

"It's just classic. Anything that's given away free, people don't attribute as much value to it," the CEO said that night. "Anything free, you won't get 100 percent people showing up. . . . If you study psychology, if people aren't paying for their therapy sessions, they feel it's not as helpful. They don't attribute as much value to it if the [therapy] is free."

Huh. Now, if free Leafs tickets are a form of therapy, exactly what disorder are they meant to treat?

🍁

CLEARLY NOT OBSESSION. How about denial? The problem is not that Leaf fans love their team too much, though it may look that way sometimes. The truth is that Leaf fans, by and large, *simply don't love their team enough.*

Yes, it is hard to believe. But let's not measure fans' passion by their eagerness to honk their horns and wave their flags when their team wins a playoff game. Instead, let's assess this so-called devotion to the team by its willingness to tolerate incompetence and profiteering.

Take the case of the Newcastle United Football Club, one of England's great sporting institutions. The parallels with Toronto's hockey club are rough, but relevant. The Magpies, as they're known, haven't celebrated around a trophy since 1969, when they won the Inter-City Fairs Cup, a forerunner of the UEFA Cup (a competition between clubs from various European leagues). It's a streak of dismay that can perhaps be considered more excruciating than Toronto's because a) soccer teams have the luxury of playing for more than one championship each year, simultaneously competing for various league and cup titles, and b) soccer fans in Newcastle take losing a lot harder than hockey fans in Hogtown.

When Mike Ashley bought the club in 2007 for approximately £134 million, he was feted as the man who might pull the club out of its historic mire. He was, after all, a self-made billionaire who parlayed a sportswear company he started as a teenager into a many-tentacled empire that included one of England's largest retailers. "The perfect football owner," cheered London's *Sunday Telegraph* upon Ashley's arrival upon the Tyne, Newcastle's storied river.

Before he purchased the club, Ashley had been known as something of a recluse.

But anonymity was clearly not an option in Newcastle, especially when Ashley eschewed the luxury owners' box for a seat among the throngs of Magpies supporters. For a while, all was well, especially after Ashley repatriated Kevin Keegan, the club's one-time manager and a former coach of England's national team, for another turn as the man in charge of the soccer operation. Keegan was hailed as a messiah on his return. But not long after, with the club's on-field results middling or worse, there were Leafian murmurs in Newcastle, stories of a board of directors, none of them career sportsmen, meddling in the on-field affairs, stories of Keegan's expertise being neutered by the know-it-all money men. Not long after—in a move that was vaguely reminiscent of, say, Pat Quinn having his general manager's title taken away from him while a neophyte was given the keys to the kingdom—Keegan's control over player transfers, European soccer's variation on team-to-team player movement, was handed to a man a generation his junior.

There were as-if-from-Toronto accusations that Ashley and his cohorts in the executive suite were only out to make money. And the fans, known as the Toon Army, got downright indignant at the goings-on. English soccer's heritage of hooliganism being what it is, Ashley said he feared for his safety and that of his family. He stopped attending games and attempted to sell the club, albeit unsuccessfully. Newcastle's fans, in various protests coinciding with Keegan's eventual exit, chanted: "We want Ashley out! We want Ashley out!" They sang: "Sack the board!" They were observed throwing tickets into the Tyne. They held up a sign that, roughly translated from the vernacular, said, "We're Supporters, Not Customers."

"It's my opinion that a manager must have the right to manage and that clubs should not impose upon any manager any player that he does not want," Keegan said in a statement confirming his resignation. "I feel incredibly sorry for the players, staff and, most importantly, the supporters."

The supporters didn't simply protest Keegan's departure. A couple of weeks after Keegan left, Newcastle's home stadium, St. James' Park, played host to its smallest crowd in more than fifteen years, its 52,000 seats scattered with about 20,000 souls. They came back, eventually—Leafs fans, in contrast, never leave (or throw their tickets into the Don River)—but the truce remains uneasy. Nobody is suggesting the owners of English premiership soccer clubs can't run their teams as they please. They do, and they mostly will; billionaires have a way of getting what they want. But certainly they must know there are lines that remain perilous to cross, no matter their net worth, and Ashley has entertained the idea of selling his storied, star-crossed team to relieve himself of the headache that comes with deciphering the ancient and unwritten codes of the rabble's expectations. Nobody is accusing English soccer fans of being ever-loyal golden retrievers, abandoned and hungry but rarely a threat to bark and bite. And surely

Ashley must envy the owners of a hockey team an ocean away who, because the beast isn't built to bare teeth, operate without a leash.

THE LEAFS DO IT AGAIN

JUNE 1989: With the Leafs employing a skeleton scouting staff that apparently avoids watching prospects who play outside a three-hour driving radius of Maple Leaf Gardens, Toronto uses its three first-round draft picks to select three members of the Belleville Bulls: Scott Thornton, Rob Pearson and Steve Bancroft. Other teams looking further afield take future all-stars Nicklas Lidstrom, Sergei Fedorov, Pavel Bure, Bill Guerin and Bobby Holik.

OCTOBER 16, 1989: The Leafs trade a 1991 first-round pick to the New Jersey Devils for Tom Kurvers. The 1991 draft yielded no end of talented players, from Eric Lindros to Peter Forsberg. The Devils used Toronto's third-overall pick to land defenceman Scott Niedermayer, who would go on to win three Stanley Cups in New Jersey and another in Anaheim.

MARCH 13, 1996: Kenny Jonsson, Sean Haggerty, Darby Hendrickson and a first-round pick (which became Roberto Luongo) go to the New York

Islanders for Wendel Clark, Mathieu Schneider and D.J. Smith. Jonsson, then 21, would go on to be a defensive anchor for most of a decade while Clark, at age 29, was less than four diminishing seasons from retirement.

Not sure if you've prepared very good questions for new Leafs GM, Brian Burke?
Don't worry, he'll let you know.

Chapter Ten
Find Hope in Brian Burke

"I still love the Leafs because I have faith that one day, one day it will happen. The city I love will be momentarily stunned and will change forever, like a middle-aged woman who realizes it's taken her forty-some-odd years to have her first orgasm."

— Adrian Leopold Ravinsky, Toronto

IN THE RECEPTION AREA of Maple Leaf Sports and Entertainment's executive offices, all glass and metal and high-tech polish, four high-definition big-screen TVs blare the feed from Leafs TV and Raptors NBA TV and Gol TV (the all-soccer channel the corporation acquired in 2009). But if you can take your eyes off the highlight loops for a moment, have a look at the vast display of trophies on the waiting-area sideboard. Standing proud watch over the premises are two Mobius Awards for excellence in "creative advertising," an award from the NHL for an "outstanding marketing campaign," and, the pièce de résistance among the heaps of hardware too extensive to detail here, a hunk of recognition from the folks at Tiffany and Company, the legendary metal-smiths who designed the world-famous icons awarded to the champions of the NFL and NBA. This particular paean to shininess is an elegant glass cylinder about the size of a pint of beer with an inscription that reads, "Tiffany and Co. Salutes The Toronto Maple Leafs . . . For Your Contribution to Hockey." Ah, yes. The coveted Tiffany Cup. If you stand on the right plot in Michigan's Mount Hope Cemetery, you can almost hear Terry Sawchuk choking on a smoke over the sad state of his old team's hardware collection. Looking at all those trophies, it is not impossible to think for a moment that the Leafs have actually *won* something on Richard Peddie's watch.

But facetiousness melts away like Zamboni slush on the other side of Brian Burke's office door. Since 1967 and the advent of the Ballard years, Leaf fans have had something to talk about at the water cooler that fans in other cities haven't: the question of whether the front office actually *wants* to win. For decades, it has been possible to dream of what the Buds might achieve if only they had the right people making the decisions. Whether it made you want to laugh or cry, the feeling has been that the team has been bungled by fools all these years.

But those jokes aren't really funny anymore. First, no one can say the new president, general manager, messiah and resident history buff doesn't want a Stanley Cup badly enough or doesn't know how to go about winning one. And second, joking about the franchise's ineptitude just doesn't seem like something the guy is going to chuckle at.

"Our fans are the greatest sports fans on the planet," says Burke. "So 1967 is huge in their minds, and mine. We have to reward some of this loyalty. They're entitled to a better return on their loyalty than we've given to them. I get it from fans all the time: *1967, 1967, 1967.* I tell 'em all the same thing: I was twelve. I also understand that my clock, the clock that started when I got here in November, and the clock the fans are on, it's not the same clock. I understand that. They want to win yesterday. But I'm not going to do it any other way just because people are impatient. What's happened since 1967 is a series of short-term fixes that didn't work. We're going to do it the right way here over the long term, and I either get to finish the job or I don't. But I'm not going to change it just because people are impatient. I'm not running for office. I don't have to be popular. I've just got to win."

As he speaks he is sitting in his corner office on the fifteenth floor of 50 Bay Street, the office tower that abuts his team's home rink. His bespoke suits and handsomely knotted ties are nowhere in evidence. He is wearing blue jeans and a plaid flannel shirt. It's an outfit suitable for, say, helping a buddy move, and certainly Burke has some heavy lifting in his near future. He has a roster, he acknowledges, "with a lot of holes to fill": the worst penalty-killing unit in the NHL, sub-par goaltending, a defensive corps that can't seem to stay healthy, and nary an all-star-calibre forward. The Leafs have made a habit of trading away the future, but what exactly does Burke have to trade? Any takers for Jason Blake? His team is scraping the bottom of the league standings. If the skate-sharpening machine blew up, things could hardly be more daunting.

But he has the luxury of at least a little bit of time, what he is calling his "honeymoon period" in Hogtown. He also has the faith of the faithful, who understand that Burke is less than two years removed from winning a Stanley Cup at the controls of the Anaheim Ducks. His 2007 Stanley Cup ring, which he keeps in a box in a drawer and happily presents to a visitor upon request, is like a talisman to keep the cynicism at bay. At least for a while.

For today, Burke is mostly sitting and talking between sips of the icy Diet Cokes he regularly pulls from the mini-fridge on the floor not far from his Spartan desk. His is a working lunch—if you call a handful of pills "lunch." Five capsules of macerated vegetables and a multivitamin, then a couple of Advils to deal with what Burke calls "old injuries," may not amount to a balanced diet. But if that's what it takes to turn things around in Toronto, even his nutritionist is unlikely to complain.

Burke, who was born the fourth of Bill and Joan Burke's ten children on June 30, 1955, in Providence, Rhode Island, came to hockey much later than most Advil-enhanced middle-agers of his ilk. His father was a corporate climber with the Sunbeam company, and he moved his ever-growing brood around the United States more than a few times. And though Brian and his siblings spent time living in Providence and Boston and Chicago as children, it wasn't until the family settled in Edina, Minnesota, when the Leafs' future GM was 12, that he was first smitten by what would become the game of his life. In fact, falling in love with hockey was just about the first thing he did in the hockey-mad state of Minnesota; he discovered the game on television, in a hotel room in Minneapolis, where his family was waiting for the moving truck to catch up to them. The tournament to decide Minnesota's state high school hockey champions was casting its annual glare. The Met Center, home to the NHL's Minnesota North Stars, was packed to capacity. Young Brian had thought of himself as a rugby man until that moment, but a glimpse of hockey changed that in a few minutes.

"I said, 'I've got to do this.' I remember being glued to the TV, saying, 'This is the coolest game. I've got to play this.' And I played the next year," he says.

He played well enough, quickly enough, to catch a keen eye. Lou Lamoriello, then the coach of Providence College, scouted a 15-year-old Burke in a high school tournament and came away unimpressed. In the opinion of a guy who would go on to become one of his era's dominant GMs, the gangly kid from Edina would never play college hockey (yes, apparently Burke was once "gangly"). A year on, when Lamoriello saw Burke play again, the big kid had filled out his scrawny frame a little, and he had also defied his prognostication. "His improvement was tremendous," Lamoriello later said. Not enough to get a hockey scholarship, but enough to deserve a shot at making the Friars as a walk-on. Still, Lamoriello—who, of course, would go on to helm the New Jersey Devils to three Stanley Cups before Burke had his first—told a young recruit named Ron Wilson that Burke had "no chance in hell" of actually making the team.

"Brian was a thug. . . . He really didn't have any talent," Lamoriello said. "But Brian came in, took charge, and earned a job on the fourth line to everyone's surprise."

Burke would eventually become Wilson's co-captain. And though Wilson was talented enough to carve out a pro career in the NHL and in Europe before his foray into the coaching ranks, Burke's athletic ascent had more modest limits. The Philadelphia Flyers signed Burke to a deal in 1977, and Bobby Clarke once summed up the impression the future Leafs GM made at the training camp: "Big. Slow. Bad player."

Burke played a season for Philadelphia's minor-league affiliate, the Maine Mariners, and he might have played more. But he was always a top student—a history major at Providence, Burke was once busted by Lamoriello for breaking curfew not to chase girls but to study in his dorm-room closet—and he'd been accepted to Harvard law school. He had already earned a one-year deferral to pursue his playing career, and spoke of petitioning for another year's leave. But Burke hung up his skates. "I think he realized that, if it came down to making a living with his body or with his brain, his brain had more to offer him," says Bill Burke, Brian's older brother.

Upon graduation, Brian worked for Boston law firms as a player agent, although he says he never liked having his loyalties divided among a roster of athletes who played for any number of different teams. (Burke is a chooser of sides.) He later apprenticed under Pat Quinn as assistant GM in Vancouver for most of five years, and got his own GM gig in 1992 in Hartford, where he achieved what he calls his best twelve-month turnaround of a roster. Drafting uber-defenceman Chris Pronger, along with Marek Malik, Nolan Pratt and Manny Legace in 1993 is not a bad start to a front-office career, and adding Sean Burke to the roster was a decent feather in his cap. But a lingering dispute with the owner eventually brought that job to an end. He found refuge in the NHL's Manhattan office as the league's chief disciplinarian.

It was in Vancouver, however, when he returned to succeed Quinn as GM, that Burke really got to work building a reputation as a guy who both got results and pissed off a lot of people in the process. In 1998–99, before Burke arrived, the Canucks finished the season second-last in the NHL. In 2002–03, the team had its best season in franchise history, and the following year wrested the Northwest Division title from the Colorado Avalanche. He also scored a spectacular coup by working the floor on draft day to put together a complex multi-team deal that brought both the Sedin twins to Vancouver—where today they are the backbone of the Canucks' offence.

You'd think a guy with a record like that would be hard to send packing, but that is just what happened. The Canucks decided not to renew Burke's contract and he spent the lockout without a home, dabbling in TV. But when play resumed he found work in Anaheim, where his touch helped transform the Ducks from contenders to champions in two years as the top hockey executive. In fairness, he did inherit a pretty impressive team from predecessor Bryan Murray. But he managed to trade Sergei Fedorov for rock-solid defenceman Francois Beauchemin (a Burkean trade if ever there was one), sign Teemu Selanne and Scott Niedermayer as unrestricted free agents, and trade for Chris Pronger, thereby ensuring that one of the best defencemen in the game would be on the ice for the Ducks at all times. He also hired coach Randy Carlyle. Though it was Murray who drafted Ryan Getzlaf,

Corey Perry and Bobby Ryan, the trio of young stars who now make up one of the most lethal first lines in the game, that Stanley Cup team had Burke's fingerprints all over it.

The job is the same no matter where the team plays, Burke says. His ongoing Toronto rebuild, if it goes according to plan, will result in a team not unlike those bruising, tenacious Ducks—a team, according to one of Burke's signature lines, possessed of "proper levels of pugnacity, testosterone, truculence, and belligerence." (Is it possible to have the right amount of, say, pugnacity, but not enough truculence?) Leaf fans may not have seen a lot of truculence lately, but they can ask Ottawa Senators fans what it looks like. A confident Sens team hardly broke a sweat on their way to winning their first Eastern Conference championship in 2007. But they still haven't recovered from the spanking they received at the hands of Burke's Ducks in the final. By the time that series was over, the Senators seemed loath to touch the puck for fear of being run over. If Leaf fans have fond memories of Gary Roberts stealing the Sens' lunch money come playoff time, chances are they are going to like Burke's edition of the team.

Just not right away. Fans may like *what* Burke is going to do with their team, but they may not like *when*. "It's not a case of 'Geez, I think this'll work, or I hope this'll work.' I *know* it'll work. And I know it's not a quick fix," he says.

Don't forget, Burke had a head-start with the Ducks. "We got lucky in Anaheim. We had a guy on our team named Rob [Niedermayer], and his brother Scott wanted to play. It wasn't because I sweet-talked Scott into wanting to sign with Anaheim. It wasn't because I'm this persuasive, smooth-talking guy. I had a brother with the right last name. But you can't rush the rebuilding process."

You also can't wait for a marquee player like Scott Niedermayer to drop into your lap (otherwise, odds are a Norris Trophy winner would have fallen out of the sky by now wearing a blue and white sweater). Surely clubs aren't paying executives millions of dollars a year to cross their fingers and hope that, by happenstance, the guy destined to win the Conn Smythe Trophy as playoff MVP en route to winning you a Stanley Cup is going to call and ask to play on your team. GMs shouldn't get to shrug and say, "Them's the breaks." If winners can say, "We got lucky," perhaps because they know a repeat performance will be no easy feat, then the losers—and there are twenty-nine of them every season in the NHL—get to say, "We got *un*lucky." Burke understands the fine line between relying on luck and taking advantage of opportunities.

"Whoever wins the Cup in any year is going to have significant luck. People stay healthy. Other teams are banged up. There's luck involved. It doesn't take away from anything. They hand you the Cup and you won a Cup. The fact you can look back and say you got lucky because you had Rob Niedermayer—I also know this, my first meeting with Rob, he said he was going to take his qualifying offer and leave at the end of the year. So I had to talk him into signing an extension before Scott would sign. So it wasn't pure luck."

❧

IN A YEAR THAT SAW DON SANDERSON, a 20-year-old player on a senior team in Whitby, Ontario, killed in a hockey fight, a lot of the carnival fun of watching men on skates punch each other in the face seemed to drain away. As the NHL started talking about changing the rules of engagement, suddenly there weren't a lot of people lining up to announce their support for "old-time hockey" and the need for players to police themselves. Don Cherry was an exception, of course. He can always be counted on to cheer for the guys who drop their mitts. Brian Burke was another. He never wavered in his defence of fist-to-face contact. "It's part of the game," he says, "and it always will be."

Say what you like about Cherry and his sometimes venomous comments, at least he plied his trade as a minor-league tussler in an era when the men were harder and the fights weren't stage-managed. If he wants to endorse fighting, at least he's been in the trenches himself. Burke, by contrast, played in the U.S. college ranks, where fighting isn't tolerated. He says he had one fight in four years as a member of the Providence

College Friars, and acknowledges that it wasn't exactly an epic bout (in fact, no punches were landed). And though he had his minor-league moments, he racked up all of 62 penalty minutes in 72 AHL games. He did fight Paul Holmgren, now GM of the Flyers, when they were playing summer hockey as teenagers: "He hit me, and it's a good thing the linesmen were holding us up," he says, "or I would have gone right down on my ass." Not exactly the Georges Laraque of his generation.

"When I talk about fighting," he admits, "it's not as an expert. [But] I do pride myself on some of the guys I fought. They were some of the toughest guys in the league that year. . . . I fought Billy Bennett, who threw punches from the next county. He would have killed me if he'd ever connected. I think when I did go, I picked the right guys and I did fine." Still, Sidney Crosby has more NHL fights under his belt than Brian Burke does.

That's not say that any of Burke's trademark truculence is anything but sincere. This is an avid bird-watcher who likes to unwind with a few good friends, a brace of trusty retrievers and a couple of Italian-made 12-gauge shotguns. This is a guy who will talk about his passion for military history for as long as you're willing to indulge his meanderings. He is enough of an aficionado to have read, in his estimation, "four or five hundred" books on the U.S. Civil War (an ancestor, Patrick Burke, fought in that conflict for the Union). And in his younger days,

Brian Burke spoke of his desire to serve his country in a capacity slightly more dangerous than, say, general manager of the U.S. national hockey team, a post he is occupying in the lead-up to the 2010 Olympics.

"Yes, if the United States goes to war again—hopefully not—but if they do in the next ten years, I'll volunteer without a problem," Burke told the *Hartford Courant* in October 1992. "They call my number, they won't have to come looking for me."

He hears mention of this quotation today and bristles.

"I'm the first generation that hasn't served in my family. The opportunity, fortunately or unfortunately, has not presented itself," he says. "What I said in that quote is if I were asked to serve, I would, and I still believe that. Now, at 53, it's easy to say that. They're probably not going to call. But I would serve. I think it's a duty you owe to your country. The quote's been misconstrued as if I said, 'Gee, I wish I could go out and fight tomorrow.' There's a war going on right now. If I really wanted to enlist, I could try. But if my country asked me, I'd go."

But the thing about Brian Burke is that he doesn't have to be misconstrued to ruffle feathers. Even when he is construed perfectly, his seemingly irrepressible opinions are sometimes enough to hurt his career. Back in 1990, Burke was summoned to Philadelphia to interview for his first general manager's job in the NHL. He spent the night before the interview at a playoff game between the New Jersey Devils and Washington Capitals. He stepped into the media room, where he was asked by a reporter if he thought Bobby Clarke, the deposed Philadelphia GM whose vacated office he was trying to claim, should have been fired.

"I said, 'No,'" Burke recalled a while later. "[Clarke] had been to the finals twice in six years, drafted reasonably well, and he's a close friend of mine. Well, the next day, I went to Philadelphia for the interview. There, in [Flyers president] Jay Snider's office, was my picture and a big headline in the newspaper: 'Burke: Clarke shouldn't have been fired.'"

He didn't get that job in Philadelphia, of course, and his willingness to share his opinion hasn't always made him popular with hockey insiders. He has publicly sparred with at least one agent—"I smell a rat with Don Meehan," Burke said a while back of the agent to a long list of NHLers. And he has been trading salvoes publicly with Kevin Lowe, the GM of the Edmonton Oilers, since 2007. During the off-season following the Ducks' Stanley Cup victory, Lowe tendered a $21-million offer sheet to Anaheim restricted free agent Dustin Penner, and Burke saw the poaching as an affront. Burke called Lowe "gutless" and accused him of running the Oilers "into the sewer." Even Craig MacTavish, then the Oilers' coach, entered the fray, calling Burke an "egomaniac" on "a crusade of self-promotion." If MacTavish's comments were punctuated by an unspoken "hear-hear" from various points around the NHL, even Burke's biggest fans probably wouldn't be surprised.

"I think a lot of people want to see Brian fail in his industry," says his wife, Jennifer Burke. "I know that's a terrible thing to say, but I think they begrudge his success to some extent. They'll never admit it, but I think some of his peers wouldn't mind seeing him taken down a peg or two."

Burke has battled, too, with members of the media who have dared raise his ire. In Vancouver, in particular, his jousting with the fourth estate reached the point where his wife, herself a radio and TV broadcaster, had to help negotiate a truce. (If anyone could be expected to understand both sides of the feud, it would be Jennifer, who first met her future husband when he was a guest on a colleague's radio show. When the couple began dating in the late 1990s, her newsroom friends would wonder aloud why she was spending time with "such an asshole.")

"We used to argue in Vancouver about his quote-unquote style with the media. I was in the media. I was, like, 'What are you doing, dude? Come on. You're not going to win. The pen is mightier than the sword,'" she says. "Brian felt that it was always in the defence of his players or his coach, so he would fight. One of his favourite sayings is, 'I didn't start the fight, but I'm going to finish it.' Back then I think he did use a lot of raw passion to get his point across. Now he's matured."

Jennifer Burke says there are times, after her husband has found himself entwined in yet another verbal throwdown with yet another combatant, when she has asked him why he so often opts for conflict.

"He has said to me, 'Jen, it's the only way I know how,'" she says. "And he always says, 'I can promise you one thing: I'll never be boring.' When you look at someone like a Kenny Holland, who has achieved what he has achieved without the brashness that surrounds Brian, you have the Kenny Holland way, which works great for him. And then you have the Brian Burke way, which pisses people off but still gets results. You have to ask yourself, as a fan of the game, as a supporter of the game, as someone who wants to see the game continue and not die, does the game need more personality or less? I see empty seats in Detroit and I don't know why. Why?"

If anyone knows what it is like to deal with Brian Burke, it may be his son Patrick, now a scout in the Philadelphia Flyers system and following his father's footsteps to law school. "There's an image of him of this big, angry man lumbering around just waiting for somebody to get in his way. And he likes that image, he cultivates that image, and there's truth to it. But there's also another side of him that the public doesn't see. . . . There is a temper, and God knows I've been yelled at enough times in my life to never want to have it happen again, but he's also got a lot of good in him, too."

❦

If there are reasons to doubt Burke, perhaps they include his glowing assessments of men who have become pariahs in the minds of a lot of informed hockey fans. And if his kind words for Richard Peddie are understandable given their working relationship—"a top-shelf businessman," he has called his boss—his unwavering support for NHL commissioner Gary Bettman can seem more than a little irrational. He has said that Bettman is the second-most intelligent person he has ever met—his father ranks first—and has called Bettman "worthy of the same respect" as Abraham Lincoln. Comparing one of the greatest American presidents to the man on whose watch the NHL's profile has dipped to unprecedented irrelevance in the US? It doesn't exactly reek of straight-shooting wisdom.

But Burke has buoyed his credibility by winning, of course, and by displaying a work ethic that is difficult to rival. In the days before the lockout that cancelled the 2004–05 season, when it became clear that the NHL was headed for a salary-cap system, Burke reached out to acquaintances in the front offices of National Football League teams that had been dealing with a capped payroll for years, and spent time studying their strategies. Bill Polian, the president of the Indianapolis Colts, had known Burke since both men were in charge of discipline of their respective leagues in the 1990s. Polian opened the Colts' books to Burke and showed him what it takes to win under a cap. Burke also spent time looking over the operations of the New Orleans Saints.

Says Burke: "The system that I have put together, the system we used successfully in Anaheim, we stole a whole bunch of that from the Colts. I didn't want to learn how to handle a cap when it came in. I spent the better part of three years studying how other teams did it. Rule number one is, you better draft well, because if you have star players, you need entry-level players that are playing, not just taking up a uniform, but contributing. If you don't have good young players, you're screwed. If you've got star players on your team—guys making $5 and $7 million—you'd better have guys who are decent players making $700,000."

He had both kinds of players when he won in Anaheim, Scott Niedermayer earning $6.75 million to anchor a backline that also got solid contributions from relative bargains like Francois Beauchemin ($1.3 million) and Kent Huskins ($625,000). And if it's been said that Burke left the Ducks with salary-cap problems that will hamper them for years to come, Burke says he would have loved to stick around to fix them.

(The reason he didn't was that the commute was killing him. He says he wouldn't agree to the contract extension on offer in Anaheim because his every-other-week trek to see his four kids on the east coast—this with two kids and a wife on the west coast—was untenable. Says Jennifer Burke: "As much as he tried to make it work for the kids and for me, you can't divide yourself up that much. He's been a workaholic as long as I've known him, and that will never change. But here you had a workaholic trying to juggle a wife and two sets of kids on two coasts. Something was going to give somewhere.")

Many in the hockey world had long foreseen that Burke's family responsibilities would end up meshing nicely with a job in Toronto. Burke's coronation as the Leafs' top hockey executive seemed preordained from around the time the team announced its search for a new leader in the wake of John Ferguson's firing in February of 2008, even after Cliff Fletcher was handed the temporary reins. But Jennifer Burke said the family was "on tenterhooks" for a few weeks between Burke's exit from Anaheim and the fateful call from Toronto on the American Thanksgiving weekend.

Says Gord Kirke, the Toronto lawyer who interviewed some thirty hockey executives as a member of the search committee that recommended Burke: "At the end of the day, you need the mental discipline, the toughness and the intellect to face [the media] every day . . . but also to deal with the board of directors, to deal with the whole culture that is the Toronto Maple Leafs. You narrow it down from that. There are a lot of great hockey people of talent who probably wouldn't shine in this market. Some of them withdrew from the candidacy because they knew this wasn't the market for them."

Burke could have put down Polian as a reference if he'd needed to. "He's got the most important ingredient for a club operator, which is fearlessness," says Polian. "He's not worried about what people are going to think or what people are going to say. He's going to make what he believes to be the right decision for the club. That's the one ingredient that I think really sets people apart. He's exceptionally smart. That's obvious from his educational pedigree, but it goes beyond just classroom learning. He's well versed in what makes people tick, in how to make decisions, in what goes into making a decision. He's the epitome. He's the guy that everyone else would like to be."

❦

MAYBE NOT *EVERYONE* WANTS to be Brian Burke. But Leaf fans will be happy if Brian Burke is Brian Burke— if the guy glowering in front of the microphones and peering down, well, truculently from the GM's box at the Air Canada Centre is everything he's supposed to be.

He's already swinging for the fences, as he makes it clear to all concerned that he's coming for John Tavares, just as he came for Pronger and the Sedins. He has shipped guys out, and made it clear that more changes are on the way. If you don't like the roster, just wait five minutes. A lot of Leafs spent the summer of 2009 staring at their phones.

There will be a lot of unfamiliar names and numbers on the sweaters when the 2009–10 season begins. Burke has already been scouring talent pools the Leafs used to scoff at. By the time his players were pulling their golf clubs out of the garage, Burke had signed a couple of US collegians. The first was Christian Hanson, the son of one of the infamous Hanson brothers from the movie *Slap Shot,* taking pains to point out that the younger Hanson is "not a meathead," and presumably does not wear foil on his knuckles. Hanson is a skilled forward educated at the University of Notre Dame, who Burke projects will be good enough to earn a place on one of the top two lines. He also signed Tyler Bozak, a Saskatoon kid who played for the University of Denver; Burke introduced Bozak as a first-line centre, which speaks to the level of in-house competition. (Then again, Hobey Baker finalist Jeff Farkas was once so highly touted by Leafs brass that they threw him into the cauldron of the second-round playoff series against New Jersey in 2000, hoping for some offence. Though he did score a goal in the series, he never put the puck in the net again for the Leafs.)

Still, while the Leafs were widely heralded for raiding campuses—even if signing college players isn't exactly the innovation it was when Mike Ilitch empowered his management team to do the same years ago— Burke acknowledged that Toronto was an attractive destination for Hanson and Bozak and perhaps others, not because it's a franchise with a storied history, but because the Leafs' talent-challenged roster provided one of the league's best opportunities for ice time. "I hope this is the last season we're the destination of choice for the US college player," Burke told reporters.

To make sure that it was, the search for useable pieces continued. When the 2008–09 season concluded, the Air Canada Centre crowd offered the seventh-worst team in the NHL a round of applause that some observers considered inexplicably hearty given what they had actually accomplished, but Burke wasn't in the building. He was on a trip to Copenhagen, where he had a meeting with a representative for Jonas Gustavsson, the best goaltender in Sweden's best league. Could Gustavsson be the answer for the Leafs at what Burke calls the game's most important position? Maybe. But goaltending wasn't the only concern. The Leafs were out of the playoffs with the calendar just days away from the fifth anniversary of their most recent postseason game. They were one of the worst defensive teams in the NHL, even though their two best assets, Tomas Kaberle and Luke Schenn, were defencemen. Yeah, they were stocking up on college-age entry-level guys, but they were without a single star, and the seventh pick in June's entry draft wasn't going to yield one.

Back on the fifteenth floor today, overlooking a city that's at least temporarily in his thrall, Burke is speaking about taking a break from his all-consuming troll for talent by throwing a line into the Gulf of Mexico. He is talking about a summertime salmon trip in B.C.'s Queen Charlotte Islands he's taken in the past with fellow veterans of the NHL executive suite like Doug Risebrough and Dave Nonis, Burke's longtime assistant GM in Vancouver, Anaheim and now Toronto; about an annual quest for pheasants with Harry Sinden, the Bruins lifer, and Glen Sather, the Rangers president, and Harley Hotchkiss, a "crack shot" in his 80s who doubles as the part owner of the Calgary Flames. Will Burke find time for golf? "No," he deadpans. "There's no fighting."

He doesn't mind fighting fish, though. "Best day I ever had fishing? When I was running the Hartford Whalers, we had a tough year, not very good. We played Tampa. I chartered a fishing boat, a 55-footer, went out all by myself, just me, the skipper and a mate and a case of beer," he says. "I caught thirty-two fish. Released a bunch. I caught dolphin fish—not Flipper, but a mahi-mahi, the ones with the big foreheads—I caught king fish, a couple of wahoo, a barracuda, a shark. I think I brought home eighty pounds of fish. And the mate probably brought home 200 pounds of fish and we released a bunch. I just hammered 'em. I got done, I was sunburned and my arms were sore from fighting the fish. It was awesome."

He smiles, sips some Diet Coke and pops an Advil at the memory.

"This business—if you don't get a break from it—will kill you," he says, and now he is talking about a hockey team in need of culling. "I'm not doing anything short term. And I think people get it. They've been around since 1967. They've seen the shortcuts. They've seen the short-term plans. They've seen the chewing gum and bailing wire, and they want a long-term approach. We want to do this the right way. We want to have a parade here, but getting to the parade is not going to be easy, and like I said, I'm not running for re-election. I'm not worried about being popular. I'm worried about winning."

What for now we'll continue to call Leafs AbomiNation is looking forward to it. We just hope there will be someone around who remembers the parade route.

THE LEAFS DO IT AGAIN

MARCH 23, 1999: Leafs trade little-used defenceman Jason Smith, then 25, to Edmonton for two draft picks that become Jonathon Zion and Kris Vernarsky. Zion never plays in the NHL; Vernarsky plays 17 NHL games, none with Toronto. Smith has played more than 1,000 NHL games, captaining teams in Edmonton and Philadelphia.

OCTOBER 1, 1999: Leafs trade Fredrik Modin to Tampa Bay for Cory Cross and seventh-round pick Ivan Kolozvary. Modin, who averages 47 points in the coming six seasons, wins a Stanley Cup with the Lightning. Cross, after a few unremarkable seasons in Toronto, has a difficult time adapting to both the post-lockout NHL and the German league, where his career ends.

MARCH 31, 2009: Leafs are mathematically eliminated from the playoffs for a franchise-record fourth straight season. Brian Burke, the president and general manager, calls it "a kick to the groin."

Epilogue

Since the day in mid-April of 2009 when Brian Burke turned a routine post-mortem on a failed Leafs season into a tour de force of bluster and blarney, beating even the most ornery Leafs debunker to the punch by assailing the club's culture of entitlement and lack of talent, the question was: Could he do anything about it?

To his credit, Burke, for the short term, set the bar high, pledging to make a run at acquiring number-one-rated prospect John Tavares. And while in the weeks that followed Burke acknowledged that progress in his pursuit of Tavares was slow—he made the act of landing the pick sound only slightly trickier than halting climate change—media reports and speculation generated hope that a late flurry of deals would land the Leafs the potential superstar they've never drafted. No such luck.

In the end, the draft came and went with the Leafs doing, er, nothing of note. The price to secure a top pick would have included the services of Luke Schenn, after all, and Burke made it clear to the world that under no circumstance was he prepared to part with his 16-point D-man. And so the GM, complaining that his counterparts with the coveted selections were reluctant to deal with him lest he pull off another of his famous draft-day heists, had to content himself with the seventh-overall pick. After he called the name of Nazem Kadri, a speedy forward from the London Knights slated to become the first Muslim to play for the team of Conn Smythe and Larry Tanenbaum, Burke went so far as to suggest Kadri had been a draft target all along. Though, to be fair, he was asked about his satisfaction with his number-seven pick while the elated teenager was sitting right beside him.

Overall, in a draft that was thick with European talent, Swedes in particular, the man who introduced "truculent" into the local lexicon drafted only North American-born players. "Pick-and-shovel men," Burke called them, without apology, even if old-timers would have told you that Burke's lopsided geographic tilt recalled the Leafs' post-expansion indifference to anything happening on the other side of the Atlantic. Otherwise the highlight of the draft was Burke getting booed and jeered by the Montreal fans as he took the podium at the Bell Centre. "I don't give a rat's ass about that," Burke said. "I will tell you this: The best hockey fans on the planet are not in Montreal, they're in Toronto. When we host this event in a couple years and Montreal goes up to pick this will seem like child's play for the booing they will get in Toronto."

See? Truculent. But failing to make a big splash doesn't mean failing to select wisely. Mark Seidel, the chief scout of the North American Central Scouting Service, gave the Leafs an A+ for their work in Montreal. Time will be the ultimate judge, and Burke plainly vowed to make the playoffs come the spring of 2010. Meanwhile, the NHL playoffs generated some incredible hockey despite the Leafs' absence. Perhaps the best came in the Eastern Conference final, when the Pittsburgh Penguins and Washington Capitals, two franchises stocked liberally with the kind of elite young talent that only comes with being really bad and then drafting well, played an epic seven-game series showcasing the talents of Sidney Crosby, Evgeni Malkin and Alexander Ovechkin. Of an eventual, peripheral sniff of a moment so rich, Leaf fans can only dream.

The broader story that dominated coverage in lieu of a Leafs playoff run was the prospect of a second NHL team invading Southern Ontario and forcing the Leafs to share some portion of the Golden (Horseshoe) Goose. The how and the when are still details that need work, given that Research In Motion co-founder Jim Balsillie's bid to rescue the Phoenix Coyotes out of bankruptcy failed to impress judge Redfield T. Baum in Arizona. But perhaps for the first time it became clear that Leafs hegemony in the world's most lucrative hockey market—an "unserved" market, in Balsillie's not-so-veiled shot at the 1967 champs—was unlikely to last much longer. There is simply too much money to be made.

Balsillie promised that if he landed the Phoenix Coyotes in Hamilton, he would make Copps Coliseum the anti-Air Canada Centre: no ties or stodginess allowed; a veritable Hockey Night at Tim Hortons. (Mind you, Balsillie's plans to renovate the circa-1985 arena, largely with public money, included an order for the construction of fifty-some concourse-level luxury boxes and twenty so-called "bunker suites" in the bowels of the arena, the latter of which would ensure, in the grand tradition of the corporate-writeoff era, that the first few rows of seating would remain empty for the opening minutes of the second and third periods while their occupants polished off their below-grade sushi platters). Meanwhile another group emerged from a growing crowd of entrepreneurs determined to capitalize on the popular notion of a second southern Ontario team. The Toronto Legacy Group unveiled a concept long on imagination, if short on specifics and cash, that called for a 30,000-seat arena, cheap tickets and vast donations to charity. All the Legacy needed, alas, was a franchise, an arena and, oh, access to the federally owned land on which they wish to build it. Far-fetched or not, the message was clear: There is a demand for another NHL team, and one that is not like the Leafs. MLSE's careful silence supported commissioner Gary Bettman's efforts to block Balsillie's backdoor maneuverings. Speculation emerged that for the right price— $50 million? $100 million?—the men who run the

Leafs could be convinced that another NHL team in their backyard wouldn't be the worst thing in the world. As always in the Leafland, everything remains for sale, but damned if the Blue and White still can't buy an important victory.

Acknowledgments

The authors would like to thank Craig Pyette at Random House Canada, who owns both a Garry Valk jersey and his own private moments of Leafs-induced joy and pain. Mostly pain. He believed in this book from the outset and was enthusiastic, patient and expert at every step thereafter.

It would be impossible to do a project like this without the insights, direct and indirect, provided by the members of the Toronto media who cover and have covered the Leafs on a daily basis since their infancy. To the many scribes and broadcasters who've worked the beat, we extend our gratitude.

We also owe an immeasurable debt to the authors of a stack of excellent books that helped form our views and enliven our text, among them *Ballard* by William Houston; *'67: The Maple Leafs, Their Sensational Victory, and the End of an Empire* by Damien Cox and Gord Stellick; *But I Loved It Plenty Well* by Allen Abel; *Hockey Night in Canada: The Maple Leafs' Story* by Foster Hewitt; *The Road to Hockeytown* by Jim Devellano and Roger Lajoie;

Lanny by Lanny McDonald and Steve Simmons; *Conn Smythe: If You Can't Beat 'Em In The Alley* by Conn Smythe and Scott Young; *Tales From The Toronto Maple Leafs* by David Shoalts; *Hockey Heartaches and Hal* by Gord Stellick and Jim O'Leary; *Hockey Is A Battle* and *Heaven and Hell in the NHL* by Punch Imlach and Scott Young; *On the Road* and *On the Road Again* by Howard Berger; *Searching For Bobby Orr* by Stephen Brunt; *The Story of Maple Leaf Gardens* by Lance Hornby; *The Leafs* by Brian McFarlane; *Centre Ice* by Thomas Stafford Smythe; *Forever Rivals* by James Duplacey; *The Best Game You Can Name* by Dave Bidini; *The Leafs* by Jack Batten; *The Canadian Hockey Atlas* by Stephen Cole; *The Meaning of Puck* by Bruce Dowbiggin; *The Death of Hockey* by Jeff Z. Klein and Karl-Eric Reif; and *Offside: The Battle for Control of Maple Leaf Gardens* by Theresa Tedesco.

Lance Hornby of the *Toronto Sun* deserves credit for preserving his tape of John Brophy's f-bomb-laced tirade circa 1988. We harvested most of the fan-generated epigraphs from the *Toronto Star*'s "Voices" forum and from the results of our own web-based invitations for comment. Thanks to all who replied.

Special thanks go to Randy Robles at the Elias Sports Bureau for his speedy statistical service; to Roy MacGregor of the *Globe and Mail,* Dave Perkins, Chris Young and Damien Cox of the *Toronto Star,* Elliotte Friedman of *Hockey Night in Canada,* Gord Miller of TSN and Pierre McGuire of multi-media superstardom for their sage guidance; to Ken Campbell of *The Hockey News* for his thoughtful read of early drafts; to Nick Garrison for his subsequent polish; to Lloyd Davis for his exceptional care; to Brian Wood for inspiring the early explorations of the idea; and to the sports editors at the *Toronto Star* and *The Globe and Mail,* Mike Simpson and Tom Maloney, for their support and patience.

Our families cannot be thanked enough, but here's a start. This book could not have been written without Margaret and Noel Grange, and Brian and the late Muriel Feschuk, parents who always made reading and writing important; or without Faeron, Avery and Ellis, and Andrea and Oscar, all beautiful reminders that other things are, too.

Many individuals willingly gave their time in interviews that helped shape this book, some of whom appear in these pages, some who do not. We are grateful to them all. Thanks, above all, to the legions of Leafs fans who follow their team with passion and loyalty. Your faith may or may not eventually be rewarded, but we admire and respect you for keeping it all the same.

Photo Credits

Every effort has been made to contact copyright holders; in the event of an inadvertent omission or error, please notify the publisher.

Introduction: *Toronto Star* File Photos/GetStock.com

Chapter One: Boris Spremo/GetStock.com

Chapter Two: courtesy of *The Globe and Mail*

Chapter Three: Canadian Press/Frank Gunn

Chapter Four: Charla Jones/GetStock.com

Chapter Five: Steve Russell/GetStock.com

Chapter Six: Jeff Goode/GetStock.com

Chapter Seven: courtesy of *The Globe and Mail*

Chapter Eight: J.P. Moczulski

Chapter Nine: Island Road Images/GetStock.com

Chapter Ten: Rick Madonik/*Toronto Star*/GetStock.com

Epilogue: courtesy of Ron Terada

Index